Reforming World Trade

The Social and Environmental Priorities

Caroline LeQuesne

**PROPERTY OF:
COMPASSION IN WORLD FARMING
INFORMATION LIBRARY
PETERSFIELD GU32 3EH
PLEASE BOOK OUT BEFORE BORROWING**

Oxfam Publications

© Oxfam UK and Ireland 1996

A catalogue record for this book is available from the British Library

ISBN 0 85598 346 9

Published by Oxfam (UK and Ireland) 274 Banbury Road, Oxford OX2 7DZ UK

Available in Ireland from Oxfam in Ireland, 19 Clanwilliam Terrace, Dublin 2.

Available in North America from Humanities Press, 165 First Avenue, Atlantic Highlands, NJ 07715-1289, USA

This book is co-published by members of the international Oxfam group in Australia, Canada, New Zealand, the USA, and the United Kingdom and Ireland. Contact addresses are printed on the back page. It is published as a contribution to public debate, and readers are invited to consider its conclusions.

Oxfam (UK and Ireland) is a member of Oxfam Internaional and is registered as a charity no. 202918

Designed and typeset by Oxfam Design Department 701/MCA/96

Set in 10/12.5 point Palatino with Franklin Gothic Book and Demi

Printed by Oxfam Print Unit on environment-friendly paper

Contents

Acknowledgements iv
Introduction 1

Chapter one: The Uruguay Round 8
    From GATT to WTO 8
    Winners and losers 10
    Unresolved issues 21

Chapter two: International trade and labour standards 28
    The garments industry in Bangladesh 28
    Codes of Conduct 40
    The role of the ILO 43
    The case for a social clause 47
    Lessons from other trade agreements 59
    The way forward 65

Chapter three: Reconciling trade and sustainable development 67
    Profits and pollution havens 67
    International trade, economic growth, and the environment 71
    The WTO: an inadequate framework for sustainable development 75
    Sustainable natural resource management 85
    Case study: promotion of a sustainable banana trade 88
    Institutional reform 91

Chapter four: An agenda for reform 94
    The case for reform 94

Notes 103

Acknowledgements

Many people, both Oxfam staff and others, have contributed to the development of this book, by sharing their experience and offering helpful criticism and advice.

I am especially grateful to Ruth Mayne for her substantial input to the analysis, particularly in chapter two. I have drawn heavily on her work on the ILO, its Conventions, and social clauses, and on her research on flexible labour markets in Chile and homeworking in the UK.

Thanks are also due to Belinda Coote and Tasneem Nahar, for information about the garments industry in Bangladesh; to staff and counterparts in the Dominican Republic; to Kevin Watkins for his ideas and valuable observations throughout the writing process; and to Charles Arden-Clarke, Senior Policy Advisor, WWF International, for particularly constructive comments and critique.

Caroline LeQuesne
Oxford, March 1996

Introduction

International trade not only gives rise to impenetrable and seemingly endless rounds of GATT negotiations and frenetic activity on the floors of commodity markets: it also has profound effects on people's livelihoods and their most basic social and economic rights. For millions of the world's poorest people, trade is involved in every aspect of their day-to-day struggle to survive. Trade can support livelihoods: production for export can generate income, employment, and foreign exchange which poor countries need for their development. But without adequate safeguards, trade can also destroy livelihoods, cause environmental destruction, or lead to unacceptable levels of exploitation.

International trade is currently integrating national economies and labour markets more tightly together as the flow of goods and services across borders expands. At the same time, the rapid expansion of foreign investment into many countries is eroding boundaries between labour markets. The overall effect is to lock producers, both North and South, into an increasingly competitive system, bringing the threat that lower social and environmental standards will increasingly be used to facilitate trade expansion.

Formidably powerful and publicly unaccountable transnational companies (TNCs) present particular problems. Their growing strength and mobility have been facilitated both by technological advances, and by the progressive withdrawal of investment controls by governments and by the GATT/World Trade Organisation (WTO). They are now increasingly able to exploit differences in social and environmental standards between countries, with a view to maximising profits, creating global production systems over which governments have little control. This carries with it the threat of a constant downward pressure on these standards as countries compete with each other to offer foreign investors the most 'favourable' conditions. Under these circumstances it is not surprising that rapid trade liberalisation is, in many areas, undermining livelihoods.

This report will make the case that world trade rules should therefore be reformed to protect people's basic rights, and to promote sustainable development.

The social and environmental costs of export expansion in Chile...

Oxfam's experience of working with poor communities in Chile offers a case in point.[1] Chile is often hailed as a shining example of the success to be won through economic liberalisation, market deregulation, and integration into global markets. The economy grew at a rate of 8 per cent in 1995, the agricultural export sector is booming, official unemployment rates are low, and wages have risen in real terms in recent years. Behind such positive statistics, however, lie serious social and environmental problems which rarely appear in official figures.

Where production of commercial export crops is dominated by large-scale producers and foreign companies, it is they, rather than the rural poor, who will receive the major benefits from trade expansion. In Chile, specialised production of fruit for export markets has emerged as an important source of foreign exchange, accounting for 13 per cent of total earnings in 1993. From 1974-1990, exports of fresh fruit grew at 25 per cent each year. Over half of fruit exports, however, are controlled by just five TNCs.

Chile's export expansion and competitive success have to a large extent been built on the basis of a cheap and flexible labour market. Research commissioned by Oxfam shows that employment growth has taken place largely in low-paid, low-quality jobs, with an increase in temporary work, sub-contracting and homework, and in the use of cheap female labour. Oxfam supports projects in the fruit export sector, where 83 per cent of the labour force is employed on a temporary basis, between 40-50 per cent of workers have no contract, and pay and conditions are among the worst in the country. Temporary workers are generally paid piece rates, are not entitled to social security benefits such as sickness and maternity payments, and have no employment protection or basic trade union rights.

Carmita is one of almost a million seasonal fruit workers in Chile. During the four-month season, she often works 16 hours a day, seven days a week. Most of the day is spent standing, with just a ten-minute break in the evening.

Despite Chile's economic success, 43 per cent of workers still earned less than the amount necessary to cover their basic needs, in 1992. As a result, although open unemployment has fallen significantly in recent years, one in three of the population were still living in poverty in 1994. Rural Chile experienced one of the most dramatic increases in inequality on record between 1987 and 1990 and overall income inequality increased further between 1992 and 1994 as wages failed to keep pace with rises in productivity. A report by the UN Research Institute for Social Development has concluded that precarious low-wage employment is now the major cause of poverty in Chile today.[2]

Chile's export success has also been based on the rapid extraction and export of natural resources under lax environmental regulations. This has brought with it correspondingly high environmental costs. One of the major problems is the intensive use of fertilisers and pesticides needed to meet the requirements of export markets. According to a former Oxfam partner organisation, AGRA, around 4 million kilos of pesticides are routinely used every year on the 220,000 hectares of land devoted to fruit production for the export market. Between 1985 and 1992 imports of pesticides grew at an annual average rate of 12.3 per cent, and by 1992 imports of agro-chemicals represented 28 per cent of total agricultural imports. Some of them, such as Paraquat, Parathion and Lindano, are among the 'dirty dozen'– some of the most toxic pesticides in the world.[3]

According to Carlos Vidal, a union leader representing fruit workers in the Aconcagua valley, the centre of the fruit export boom in Chile:

The water's full of pesticides from the fruit production. This area used to be famous for water melons and now they don't grow properly any more. They chuck fertilisers and pesticides everywhere – it doesn't matter that the earth is dead because the fruit trees thrive artificially.

Workers often have to work in the fields immediately after crops have been sprayed, or sometimes even during spraying, without adequate protective clothing; while women working in the confined spaces of packing plants and greenhouses are particularly exposed to the damaging effects of pesticides. These include skin complaints, nervous disorders, muscular wasting, sterility, nausea, a higher incidence of miscarriages, and an increased rate of malformed babies. In the regional hospital at Rancagua, in one of the main fruit producing areas, investigations have shown that of the 90 babies born with a range of neural tube defects in the first 9 months of 1993, *every one* was the child of an agricultural worker from the fruit farms. The Rancagua figure for these defects is three times the national average.

Carmita is in poor health and has been told that she will soon be unable to work. She suffers from persistent skin complaints and kidney infections, illnesses common among seasonal workers in the fruit sector, which are believed to be linked to constant exposure to pesticides. The chemicals also have irreversible effects on wildlife, and contaminate rivers, underground springs, and soils.

...and the costs of increased competition in the UK

By driving down labour costs, and keeping environmental standards low, Chile has been able to remain competitive in international markets. Some 8,000 miles away, in the north of England, comparable economic forces are at work. The UK clothing and textile industry has been facing increasing competition, both from Europe and from countries in the South. In a labour-intensive industry like this, one of the easiest ways of staying competitive is to cut labour costs. Companies have taken advantage of the government's weak employment legislation to sub-contract certain stages of the production process to sweat-shops and homeworkers at very low wages. As most small businesses and homeworkers are classified as self-employed, or not registered at all, they are rarely covered by collective bargaining agreements or government legislation. This legal loophole means that large numbers of people, often women or immigrants, are working for dismal pay, with no job security and negligible employment rights, and in poor conditions.

Although 'homeworking' can be lucrative for highly skilled consultants in service industries, many traditional homeworkers are unskilled, and therefore vulnerable to exploitation. The majority of them are women, and many of them are caught between the need to earn and the need to be at home to look after children. Homeworking is often portrayed as the ideal solution for women to achieve both goals but in reality the piece-work rate is usually minimal, and women have to work so hard that they have little time or energy for child care. Homeworkers frequently suffer poor health and safety conditions. The hours are long and irregular, the work monotonous and isolating.

As one homeworker in the garments industry recently reported:

I have no advantages by working from home except that I can look after my children. I am being paid a very low piece-work rate, and have never received work on a regular basis. My two children are suffering from asthma and I think it is because of my work. Our heating and lighting costs have more than doubled...Once or twice I have asked my employer regarding regular work and a pay increase, but he said, 'I am only going to give this, take it or leave it.' With no choice I have to carry on because I know that all employers are the same. The thing that really hurts me is that the employers treat us like slaves, not workers.[4]

A survey by the West Yorkshire Homeworking Unit in 1992 found that the average estimated hourly rate of pay for homeworkers was £1.16. The highest rate was £3.00 per hour for clothing work, with some workers receiving 50 pence or less per hour. This compares with average earnings in the West Yorkshire region of £6.23 per hour.[5]

In a world where labour markets are becoming increasingly integrated through the mechanism of international trade and investment, the challenge is to prevent such experiences from becoming the norm as international competition threatens to drive standards down both in the industrialised countries, and in the South.

This task is made even more urgent by the proliferation of regional free-trade agreements, several of which involve huge swathes of the world. There are plans for a free-trade area covering all of North and South America. The USA and EU are discussing a transatlantic free-trade area, the EU has recently concluded a free-trade agreement with MERCOSUR (the customs union linking Brazil, Argentina, Uruguay, and Paraguay), and the Asia-Pacific Economic Co-operation (APEC) forum envisages free trade by 2020 among its 18 members, which include the USA, Japan, and China. Many regional agreements envisage a rate of liberalisation both faster and broader than the WTO.[6]

This report focuses on the WTO, and makes the case that it has so far failed to create a viable framework for the social and environmental regulation of international trade. Although the Agreement signed at the end of the Uruguay Round includes a commitment to promoting sustainable development, its rules are focused almost entirely on the narrower objective of trade expansion. Developing country governments have reacted strongly against the suggestion that minimum social and environmental standards should be established within the WTO, fearing that this could encourage protectionist action. They point out, with considerable justification, that poverty is the real cause of low standards, in that poorer countries lack the financial and administrative capacity to implement, monitor, and enforce legislation; and they claim that access to Northern markets is vital to raising standards. At the same time, however, the world cannot afford a global trading system which subordinates all other considerations to trade expansion.

Oxfam believes that the WTO should therefore be reformed to create an international regulatory system which protects the environment and safeguards people's basic rights, without jeopardising legitimate trade interests. The WTO's first Ministerial

Introduction

Meeting in Singapore in December 1996 offers a significant opportunity to review the links between trade and environment, and trade and labour, and therefore to promote sustainable development.

The report is in four chapters: the first provides an overview of the recently completed Uruguay Round, and demonstrates how the greatest economic benefits resulting from the Agreement will go to the industrialised nations. At the same time, the social and environmental costs of trade liberalisation mean that a growing number of people in both North and South face the risk of increased marginalisation. The chapter also examines those issues which were left out, or only partially addressed, during the Uruguay Round negotiations, and focuses in particular on two areas: trade and labour standards, and trade and environment. The second and third chapters use case studies from Oxfam's own programme experience to make the case for minimum social and environmental standards in international trade agreements, and the final chapter offers an agenda for reform, with recommendations both for the Singapore Ministerial Meeting, and for the longer term.

CHAPTER ONE: THE URUGUAY ROUND
From GATT to WTO

On 15 April 1994, trade ministers from 117 governments met in Marrakesh, Morocco, to sign the *Final Act Embodying the Results of the Uruguay Round of Multilateral Trade Negotiations*. The Marrakesh meeting was the culmination of more than seven years of negotiations under the General Agreement on Tariffs and Trade (GATT). The 'Final Act', which entered into force on 1 January 1995, comprises over 400 pages of principal text, with another 18,000 pages of market access details, and it extends multilateral trade rules to almost every area of international commerce. Two sectors which had previously been outside GATT rules, agriculture and textiles, were brought within the rules-based system, while comprehensive agreements were also reached on investment, trade in services, and trade-related aspects of intellectual property.

The Uruguay Round broke new ground in bringing international trade rules to bear on areas that had previously been considered the sovereign domain of national governments. Previous international trade negotiations had focused primarily on tariff-cutting, but with customs duties at generally low levels for industrial goods in developed countries, the focus of the Uruguay Round was broadened to include the wide range of non-tariff barriers which are used to protect domestic producers.

In addition, the Uruguay Round resolved to replace the General Agreement on Tariffs and Trade (GATT), still a provisional legal entity nearly half a century after its creation in 1947, with a much more powerful and permanent World Trade Organisation (WTO). The main functions of the WTO, which currently (February 1996) has 119 members, are:

- to supervise implementation of the Uruguay Round accords;
- to act as a forum for ongoing multilateral trade negotiations;

- to settle disputes using a strengthened semi-judicial disputes procedure which no longer allows trade offenders to block decisions against them.

To join the WTO a prospective member has to accept every part of the Uruguay Round Agreement, treating it as a 'single undertaking'. This marks a significant departure from the GATT, many of whose provisions were contained in voluntary codes and practices. Although the WTO attempts to reach decisions by consensus, where this is not possible it adheres to the principle of one-member, one-vote (as did its predecessor, the GATT), making it unique among multilateral institutions. (Both the IMF and the World Bank operate a weighted voting system, with voting power linked to the amount of money contributed to the budget.) However, if the history of the GATT is any indication, there is still likely to be a notable imbalance within the WTO in power relations between the developed and the developing countries. The agenda of the Uruguay Round is itself testament to the superior bargaining power of the industrialised countries, who succeeded in getting issues like investment and intellectual property rights onto the agenda, in spite of the initial opposition of Southern governments, while issues of concern to some of the poorest countries in the South, such as progress on commodity prices, were notably absent from the negotiations.

Had the Uruguay Round failed to result in an agreement, the industrialised countries could well have descended into cycles of trade retaliation and cross-retaliation, a process in which developing countries, with their limited retaliatory powers, would almost certainly have suffered. The agreement which has emerged, however, is weighted very firmly in favour of the industrialised nations and the transnational corporations (TNCs) which are mostly based there.

Winners and losers

According to the triumphant declaration of Peter Sutherland, then Director-General of the GATT, on the eve of the Marrakesh signing ceremony, all countries will emerge as winners from the Uruguay Round. Major international institutions like the World Bank, OECD, and the GATT have justified the whole Round in terms of the huge financial gains which it is apparently going to yield. Estimates of the increases in annual world trading income to be generated by the Agreement by 2002 have risen in dizzying leaps and bounds, starting at $213 billion according to a World Bank-OECD study, rising to $234 billion in a subsequent GATT secretariat analysis, and culminating in revised claims of some $500 billion by 2005.[7]

However, the corresponding social and environmental costs of the Agreement have not figured in any of the official calculations. Moreover, even by their own evidence, these estimates look a good deal less impressive when distributional considerations are taken into account. According to the World Bank-OECD study, for example, less than one-third of the gains it predicted would go to the South, with China and a few upper-income South-East Asian countries the principal beneficiaries. The lion's share of the increase, an estimated $80 billion, would accrue to the European Union, and the US national income would rise by $19 billion. Sub-Saharan Africa, the world's poorest region, would actually lose income – an estimated $2.6 billion, due in part to a loss of preferences in the European market.

Distributional effects take place within countries, as well as between them, of course, with some groups of people likely to gain or lose much more from increasing trade liberalisation than others. This is particularly the case for poor producers. Without far-reaching structural reforms, including agrarian reform, to enable the poor to participate in markets on more equitable terms, the distribution of benefits from commercial markets will largely reflect existing inequalities in power and opportunity. For example, while Brazil is expected to see a significant expansion of soya cultivation under the Uruguay Round Agreement, the main beneficiaries are likely to be powerful commercial interests. Brazilian soya cultivation is dominated by large landholdings, and has historically been associated with displacement of smallholder producers, and deforestation.

Many women in developing countries may also see few of the benefits of trade liberalisation, because they are mainly involved in trade in the informal economy. This is partly because of the barriers they face to entering the formal employment market, including gender discrimination, and their lower levels of education, and limited mobility. Women living in poverty are often so disadvantaged in terms of their access to training, producer services, and infrastructure generally, that they are unable to take advantage of liberalisation measures. Narrow economic growth strategies, including strategies to facilitate trade liberalisation, therefore do not necessarily advance these women's interests at all.

For those women who are in formal industrial employment, a combination of trade-related economic measures and trends in international trade have brought an expansion of employment opportunities. However, as we shall see in the case of garment workers in Bangladesh, examined in chapter two, these changes generate a complex set of gains and losses. While employment is crucial for these women, and has in some cases brought them an income and a new-found independence, status, and self-confidence, it is important not to over-estimate the long-term impact. There is a very real danger that, for as long as women have only their cheap, unskilled labour to offer, their working conditions will deteriorate, the insecurity of their jobs will increase, and their standard of living will remain low.[8]

As for the distribution of gains and losses between nations, the agreements reached demonstrate that the focus of the Uruguay Round was on issues primarily of concern to the industrial countries, such as intellectual property and investment. Long-standing problems facing primary commodity exporters, however, were not dealt with, while agricultural over-production in the North, and discriminatory protectionism, were only partially addressed. These areas are examined in more detail in the following sections.

Primary commodities

Although primary commodities are of diminishing significance in international trade flows, they are of great importance to some of the world's poorest countries and people. Some 30 countries in Africa and 18 in Latin America depend on primary commodity exports for more than half their export earnings. Yet for well over a decade, primary commodity exporters have faced the worst depression in world markets since the 1920s. Between 1980 and 1993, prices for non-oil primary commodities fell by more than half in relation to prices for manufactured goods. The estimated annual loss to developing countries over this period was around $100 billion: more than twice the total flow of aid in 1990.

Falling commodity prices also have significant environmental effects by reducing the scope for internalising the environmental costs of production and trade (i.e. incorporating the costs of environmental degradation associated with commodity extraction or production into the market price). While higher commodity prices are not a panacea for environmental problems, falling prices bring particularly adverse effects. In particular, the underpricing of natural resources and environmental goods leads to inequitable, wasteful, and environmentally destructive patterns of production and consumption – in direct contradiction to Agenda 21's call on governments to ensure that 'commodity prices...reflect environmental, social, and resource costs'.[9]

Inadequate investment and lack of international support for diversification away from commodity dependence is compounded by Northern protectionism. One of the most effective ways for developing countries to escape dependence on volatile primary commodity markets is to add value to their exports through local processing. This practice is actively discouraged by the industrialised countries, however, who impose import tariffs which rise with the level of processing.

The practice of tariff escalation not only prevents poorer countries from diversifying away from primary commodities into processing activities, but also further intensifies environmental pressure. Japan and the EU, for instance, both impose a higher tariff on plywood than on logs. The aim, in both cases, is to protect powerful domestic timber industries. The effect is to increase the environmental degradation in exporting countries, since logs have a lower unit value than plywood, and more would have to be exported to generate the equivalent amount of foreign exchange.

Some evidence also suggests that processing activities themselves tend to be less environmentally damaging than extraction. An Austrian study recently found that mining bauxite to make alumina uses about 10 per cent of the total energy used in making the final aluminium product, and produces 90 per cent of the wastes while accounting for only 10 per cent of the profits. The second stage, processing alumina into raw aluminium, uses about 80 per cent of the energy and produces 9 per cent of the wastes, while accounting for 20 per cent of the profits. In contrast, the final stage of manufacturing refined metal goods generates 70 per cent of all profits while requiring only 10 per cent of the total energy use and producing only 1 per cent of the wastes.[10] The primary producer thus gains the least benefit, and suffers the most environmental pollution from wastes.

Developing countries could reasonably have expected significant progress in addressing these issues during the Uruguay Round. They were disappointed. Tariff escalation in some of the areas of most relevance to them, including beverages, oilseeds, and fish, will continue at between 8 per cent and 26 per cent, reducing the benefits of the Agreement for the world's poorest countries. Moreover, for the poorest commodity producers in sub-Saharan Africa, there are justifiable fears that the Uruguay Round Agreement will jeopardise trade prospects in European markets. This is because the Agreement will lower tariffs for all countries, thereby reducing the trade preferences currently offered by the

EU to Africa under the Lomé Convention.[11] Projections by the OECD in 1994 suggested that the resulting loss in foreign exchange earnings from 2002 could amount to over $2 billion annually for sub-Saharan Africa (including South Africa).

Protectionism in manufactured goods

If developing countries are to reduce their dependence on primary commodities and expand their exports of manufactured goods, they clearly need access to markets. However, the Uruguay Round only partially addressed the huge number of trade barriers which they face. While their share of exports entering industrial country markets duty free will double, the proportion attracting tariffs of 10 per cent or more will remain relatively high – and far higher than for goods traded between the industrial countries themselves.

In theory, WTO rules require all countries to respond to liberalisation by their trade partners by offering equivalent measures. This has not been happening, partly because developing countries have been liberalising their economies unilaterally, often as a result of structural adjustment policies (SAPs), as well as under GATT obligations, in which case the industrialised countries are technically not required to reciprocate. In the Philippines, for example, average tariffs were reduced from over 41 per cent in 1981 to around 20 per cent in 1995 under SAPs, while import restrictions were removed from 2,800 product categories. There have been no comparable reductions in the industrialised countries.

Poor countries have also faced an array of non-tariff barriers (NTBs): contrary to a commitment made at the beginning of the Uruguay Round to 'roll back' such restrictions, they actually increased during the 1980s. Evaluating the implications of the Uruguay Round Agreement for NTBs is made difficult by the very different interpretations which have been placed on its provisions. It is likely that many NTBs will remain intact, albeit under a different guise. While so-called 'voluntary export restraints' will be phased out, for instance, other 'safeguard' measures will probably fill the gap. Other departures from WTO rules will either be phased out over a long period or left partially intact.

Nowhere is this better illustrated than in the phase-out of the Multi-Fibre Arrangement (MFA), the most significant NTB which has faced the world's poorest countries for over 20 years. The MFA was originally introduced in 1974, supposedly as a 'temporary' departure from GATT principles, in order to allow industrialised countries to adjust their own domestic textile industries to Third World imports by imposing bilateral quotas. In practice, these were both arbitrary and discriminatory. For most Southern countries, it has also been very damaging, since textiles and clothing account for a quarter of all manufacturing exports from the South. The overall cost of the MFA to developing countries has been estimated at around $50 billion a year – about equal to the total flow of development assistance provided by Northern governments.

Under the Uruguay Round Agreement, it is to be phased out over a ten-year period. Tariffs will also be lowered. This has been hailed as one of the principal gains for developing countries. But the Agreement on textiles is heavily 'end-loaded', with most of the benefits coming at the very end of the ten-year period. It also contains a provision allowing importing countries to take 'safeguard' measures under certain circumstances to protect their own industries, including both tariff increases and restrictions on the quantities of imports. Furthermore, as we shall see in chapter two, it is by no means clear that all Southern countries will automatically benefit from the phase-out, as it is currently constituted.

Agriculture

The Uruguay Round negotiations were dominated by the issue of agricultural trade, which was brought within the GATT Agreement for the first time. The industrialised countries could have taken this opportunity to introduce thoroughgoing reforms of their wasteful and inequitable agricultural policies, typified by the EU's Common Agricultural Policy, which has been responsible for massive subsidised overproduction, bringing devastating effects for some Southern countries.

With surpluses mounting throughout the 1980s and early 1990s, the EU and US indulged in a strategy of out-subsidising each other in order to expand market share. The consequences were felt most sharply by developing countries, who saw world prices fall to their lowest level in real terms since the Great Depression. Non-subsidised exporters were hit hardest: Argentina saw its export earnings drop by 40 per cent between 1980 and 1987 as a result of falling prices for cereals and oilseeds. Subsidised exports also undermined rural livelihoods by flooding local markets with cheap imported food.

The Uruguay Round's Blair House Agreement on Agriculture, which was hailed as the start of a new era in world agricultural trade, claimed to change all this. In reality, the results are considerably less impressive, since the US and EU agreed a system of permissible subsidies which enabled them to maintain current levels of production and exports.

Briefly summarised, the Agreement has three parts: a reduction in domestic income support by 20 per cent; a reduction in the volume of subsidised exports by 21 per cent and in the value of such exports by 36 per cent; and the conversion of all import barriers into tariffs. However, because of the reference years chosen, against which these commitments will be measured, both the US and EU were able to announce that their obligations had already been met, and there would be no further subsidy cuts.

Developing countries were given some concessions: the least developed countries are not required to implement the Agreement, while the others are only obliged to make cuts of two-thirds those specified for other countries (for example, cuts in value of subsidised exports of 24 per cent instead of 36 per cent), and have ten years to do so instead of six. But the new obligation on them to reduce restrictions on agricultural imports by 13 per cent over the lifetime of the Agreement will further exacerbate the food security problems they already face. In many areas, this is likely to intensify the trend towards increased rural unemployment, with its corollary of rural–urban migration, reduced production of basic food staples, and deteriorating welfare.

Parallel developments in Mexico under the NAFTA (North American Free Trade Agreement) offer an insight into what might be anticipated. In Mexico, maize accounts for almost two-thirds of agricultural production in some areas of the country, where millions of households depend for their survival on farming steep, ecologically fragile hillsides using traditional methods of cultivation. Under the NAFTA Agreement, restrictions on US maize imports are being progressively withdrawn, along with price support to Mexican farmers. This is threatening the viability of millions of Mexican smallholdings. Average yields in Mexico are less than a quarter of those in the US, where farmers benefit not only from production subsidies (which account for one-third of the value of maize output), but also from a wide range of irrigation and marketing subsidies. It has been estimated that fewer than one in ten Mexican maize producers could compete in an unprotected market, leading to predictions that up to 2.4 million peasant producers and their families could be forced off the land.

Already it is clear that it is the poorest who will lose most from the Blair House Agreement. This is not entirely surprising, given that the poorest countries – where agriculture accounts for as much as two-thirds of employment – were not even consulted about its final text. The Agreement is, in practice, a bilateral agreement negotiated in confidence by the EU and US, where agriculture represents less than 5 per cent of national income and employment.

The regulation of TNCs

The real winners from the Uruguay Round are the transnational corporations, who have seen their powers and scope increase on a phenomenal scale. The 100 largest TNCs control over one-third of the stock of foreign investment, while 40 per cent of world trade takes place *within* companies.[12] General Electric, General Motors, and Ford have between them assets roughly double the GDP of Mexico; while the ten largest TNCs control assets which represent three times the total income of the world's poorest 38 countries (excluding China and India), with a population of over one billion people. The influence of these companies on the outcome of the Uruguay Round is particularly reflected in the agreements on intellectual property, services, and investment, where the rights of developing country governments in relation to foreign investors have been severely eroded.

Trade Related Intellectual Property Rights (TRIPS)

The insistence, on the part of the industrialised countries, that TRIPS be considered in the Uruguay Round is a classic example of double standards. While the Uruguay Round Agreement and the WTO are supposed to promote trade liberalisation and free trade flows, the TRIPS Agreement actually tightens monopoly control over technology and reduces the opportunities for new commercial rivals.

The Agreement is clearly biased towards the interests of Northern TNCs which control over 90 per cent of the world's patents. It effectively requires developing countries to enforce a patent system modelled on those of the US and the EU, and extends the period of patent protection for substantially longer than existing measures provide for in many developing countries.[13] There are very real concerns that, by rewarding monopoly through enhanced royalty collection, it will also cause the costs of technology transfer to rise, once again penalising developing countries.

Some of the most significant effects of the Agreement will be felt by local communities. In October 1992, a 500,000 strong rally of farmers in Karnataka forced the issue of trade related intellectual property rights (TRIPS) onto the political agenda. They were protesting against the proposed introduction of TRIPS into the Uruguay Round, fearing that it would rob them of their freedom to use, reproduce, and modify their seeds and plant material.

Under the new Agreement, WTO members are required to provide for the protection of plant varieties either through patents, or through an effective national system of royalty collection. This could lead to companies being able to pursue claims on patented seeds with the full weight of international trade law, and the implicit threat of sanctions against governments, behind them. As a result, farmers could be penalised for saving seeds for planting in future seasons, or for exchange with other farmers.

Furthermore, the Agreement recognises only private rights and makes no provision for the protection of intellectual property which is held communally, such as traditional knowledge of plants or seeds. Once genetic material has been modified, no matter how slightly, it can be patented by corporations or individuals, who thus gain all the financial benefits. An individual or company can collect a plant from a developing country, modify it or isolate a useful gene, and patent a new plant variety or product that contains it, without having to make any payment to the communities whose traditional knowledge enabled the plant to be identified in the first place. Farmers in developing countries will have to pay high charges for the new seeds, pesticides, and pharmaceuticals developed from their genetic resources.[14]

The TRIPS Agreement will have far-reaching environmental impacts, too. By loading incentives for the protection of genetic diversity in favour of industry rather than local people, it is likely to promote forms of breeding that encourage uniformity rather than diversity; and by reducing farmers' access to good seed, the Agreement is likely to have, in the words of a Friends of the Earth report, 'widespread and irreversible impacts on traditional agricultural systems'; and it clearly conflicts with the goals of the Biodiversity Convention by preventing or discouraging the conservation of agricultural and plant diversity.[15]

Foreign direct investment

Foreign direct investment (FDI) can play a significant role in the development process, through employment creation, training, and the transfer of technology. However, the terms on which such investment takes place are being increasingly biased in favour of the corporate interests behind it. Investment patterns are also extremely uneven, with just a handful of Southern countries receiving the bulk of FDI.

The Agreement on Trade-Related Investment Measures (TRIMS) will not allow developing country governments to insist, as a condition of market access, that foreign companies meet minimum requirements for using local materials in the production process. Governments will no longer be able to oblige these firms to export a specific share of their products, or limit their import of component parts. The WTO Agreement on Trade in Services (GATS) separately addresses issues relating to companies operating in the services sector. Under GATS, national governments may not restrict the entry of firms into sectors such as advertising, banking, and insurance which operate in other GATS member states. Other aspects of investment practice which benefit TNCs at the expense of poorer countries, such as transfer pricing, restrictive business practices, and excessive profit repatriation, were conspicuous by their absence from the Uruguay Round agenda.

Unresolved issues

One of the most important tasks of the first Ministerial Meeting of the WTO in Singapore at the end of 1996 is to review progress made to date in implementing the Uruguay Round Agreement. This in itself will be a huge undertaking. Many other issues, some new, some unresolved from the Uruguay Agreement, are also jostling to find space on the Singapore agenda. Chief among them are investment and competition policy, labour standards, and further work on trade and environment.

Investment

Scarcely before the ink was dry on the Uruguay Round Agreement, which accords foreign investors formidably wide-ranging and unprecedented powers, a new initiative was announced which will extend their scope still further. The OECD stated in a communiqué in May 1995 that it was to start work on a free-standing Multilateral Agreement on Investment (MAI), to be open to both OECD members and non-members alike, with an estimated completion date of summer 1997. This would go much further than the TRIMS Agreement, which essentially prevents national governments from imposing trade-related restrictions on investments by foreign companies. The MAI, which is being promoted most strongly by the EU, would remove all remaining national policy tools for regulating foreign investment and TNC activities. It would 'guarantee generally free entry and establishment for foreign investors, full national treatment for established investments and high standards of investment protection'.[16]

The WTO Council for Trade in Goods, at their five-year review in 2000, is due to consider whether TRIMS 'should be complemented with provisions on investment policy and competition policy'.[17] The EU's strategy appears to be to bring forward by three years the possible negotiation of an investment agreement under the WTO by proposing to have the subject added to the agenda by the WTO trade ministers at their December 1996 meeting in Singapore. The fact that some of the major industrialised countries have chosen to begin their own negotiations on investment within the OECD rather than in the WTO presents a major challenge to the multilateral trading system. It also further marginalises the UN's role in global economic and social issues.[18]

The EU's proposals are based on a number of principles. These include:
- Foreign companies should have the legal right to invest and operate competitively in all sectors of the economy.
- Host governments should treat foreign investors as least as well as national investors.
- Only transparent, narrowly defined, and well-justified exceptions from the general right of entry for foreign investment should be permitted.
- No new restrictions should be introduced, and any area under treaty obligation gradually liberalised.

Foreign investment can be of great benefit, provided that it is integrated into an appropriate policy context. Governments should continue to have the right to regulate the terms and conditions for the entry and operation of foreign investment in various sectors of the national economy. It is a particularly critical issue for developing countries, since control of foreign investment is essential in order to develop domestic capacity and allow local enterprises to become more competitive.

The proper place for any negotiations on investment is within the UN, where the rights and obligations of both foreign investors as well as of governments and their citizens can be considered in an open and transparent way.[19]

International trade and labour standards

Another issue which is likely to be discussed at Singapore is international trade and labour standards. In Marrakesh, the signatories to the WTO Agreement could not agree on any reference to a social clause. All that could be agreed was a commitment to discuss 'suggestions for the inclusion of additional items on the agenda of the WTO's work programme' (para 8 (c) (iii) of the Decision on the Establishment of the Preparatory Committee for the WTO). There was, however, reference to the importance attached by certain delegations to the relationship between trade and internationally recognised labour standards in the conclusions of the Chair of the Trade Negotiations Committee.

Identifying a link between trade and labour standards is nothing new, however. The preamble to the ILO Constitution, written in 1919, states that 'the failure of any nation to adopt humane conditions of labour is an obstacle in the way of other nations which desire to improve the conditions in their own countries.' This logic was taken further by the 1947 UN Conference on Trade and Employment, which attempted to extend the principles of the Bretton Woods framework to international trade. Article 7 of the resulting Havana Charter is extremely explicit in making the link between international trade and labour standards:

The Members recognise that unfair labour conditions, particularly in production for export, create difficulties in international trade, and, accordingly, each Member shall take whatever action may be appropriate and feasible to eliminate such conditions within its territory.

The International Trade Organisation (ITO), for which this Charter was drafted, never came into being. But if the point that unfair labour conditions can 'create difficulties' in international trade was compelling to the authors of that Charter nearly 50 years ago, it is even more relevant in today's increasingly interconnected global economy.

The suggestion that there can be and should be thresholds for participating in the international trading system is also not new. Trade rules and restrictions are already used to prevent the theft of intellectual property, while provisions for banning imports made by prisoners, and for taking measures to protect some aspects of the environment, already exist under GATT Article XX. There is no reason why similar protection could not be provided for a wider range of labour and environmental principles.[20]

Trade and environment

In order to demonstrate its concern with environmental issues, in 1971 the GATT set up a working party on Environmental Measures and International Trade (EMIT). In fact, it had precisely the opposite effect, since it failed to meet for over 20 years. Not until the end of 1991, at the instigation of the European Free Trade Association, did it hold its first meeting.

New life was breathed into the consideration of trade and environment concerns when the Uruguay Round members took the decision in 1994 to set up a new Committee on Trade and Environment (CTE). Its mandate is to make 'appropriate recommendations on whether any modifications of the provisions of the multilateral trading system are required, compatible with the open, equitable and non-discriminatory nature of the system' in order to make trade and environmental policies mutually supportive.

The Committee's agenda currently includes multilateral environmental agreements, exports of domestically prohibited goods, charges and taxes for environmental purposes, ecolabelling, and the effects of environmental measures on trade. What it does not consider is the effect of trade measures on the environment, and in particular the impact of the Uruguay Round on prospects for sustainable development.

Oxfam's experience is that livelihoods – indeed, survival – for the world's poorest people depend fundamentally on the wealth of the natural environment and on resources such as soils, trees, and water. Working in partnership with community groups to combat poverty in over 70 countries of the world, Oxfam has seen at first hand how unregulated international trade can lead to environmental degradation, which in turn deepens poverty.

As these concerns become more and more inter-related, it is becoming essential to see them as one problem. Trade and environment issues therefore cannot be addressed in isolation: development issues must also be considered. A narrow perspective on trade and environment which misses out an analysis of poverty and development risks becoming part of the problem, not part of the solution. For this reason, during the review of the CTE's work in Singapore, ministers should take the opportunity to extend its terms of reference to encompass the broader concept of sustainable development, as outlined below in chapter three.

This should not prove to be incompatible with the WTO's mandate since, in theory, the WTO is already committed to the principle of sustainable development. Its stated objectives include 'allowing for the optimal use of the world's resources in accordance with the objective of sustainable development'; 'raising standards of living'; and 'ensuring full employment'.[21] The WTO should not study these issues in isolation, however, but in collaboration with appropriate intergovernmental agencies (including UNEP, UNDP, UNCTAD, and the CSD), and should also seek the advice and experience of non-governmental organisations (NGOs) and citizens' groups.

The effects of trade liberalisation on social and environmental standards

Under certain conditions, trade liberalisation can have a positive impact on labour and environmental conditions through a more efficient allocation of resources and increases in productivity, leading to social development and higher wages. It can also contribute towards higher economic growth and inward investment, and create resources which can be used for environmental protection. None of these impacts is automatic, however; they depend rather on certain kinds of intervention.

In brief, there are three main aspects to the relationship between trade policies and environmental and labour issues. First, pressure for deregulated trade, if unchecked, can lead to the degradation of the environment and the exploitation of workers. Second, if environmental and labour regulations are lax or weakly enforced, this can lead to a downward spiral of standards, as foreign investment seeks out the lowest production costs. Third, the existing rules governing international trade can themselves prevent or discourage governments from taking measures to safeguard labour and environmental standards. It is these relationships which this report will now examine in more detail, with a view to proposing recommendations on labour and environmental standards for consideration both in Singapore and in the longer term.

The following chapter starts with a case study of the garments industry in Bangladesh, and examines how global economic integration and growing competition are pitching garment workers around the world into competition with each other, exerting downward pressure on wages and conditions, and increasing job insecurity: employment creation in one country often means job losses in another. It will also set out a range of measures to address these problems, from codes of conduct, to international standards, and finally international regulation.

One of the easiest ways to remain competitive in labour-intensive industries is to cut labour costs.[22] This can be achieved by relocating factories to regions with abundant (often female) labour reserves, with weak labour laws and lax enforcement. Or it can be achieved by sub-contracting production to sweatshops and home-workers, at home or overseas. This allows companies to evade labour regulations and collective bargaining agreements and maintain flexibility in the face of rapidly changing markets. Both strategies are common in the international garments industry.

A similar dynamic can be observed with regard to environmental standards. Countries with weak, or lax enforcement of, environmental standards have a competitive advantage in the global market-place, and put pressure on other countries to reduce, or at least not improve, the rigour of their own environmental requirements. In chapter three, drawing on experience of our project partners in Mexico, we outline the environmental costs of this competitive pressure.

Moreover, current rules for international trade liberalisation often entail market access agreements which can be used to override environmental regulations. Using a case study of shrimp farming in the Philippines, we make the case that WTO rules should be changed to enable countries to impose consumption or import taxes on the grounds of unsustainable production, and in extreme cases to prohibit imports or exports. Finally, a case study focusing on the social and environmental costs of banana cultivation, and on the difficulties facing attempts to promote preferential access for fairly and sustainably produced bananas, will demonstrate in more detail the need for WTO rules to be reformed to permit countries to discriminate between imports on the basis of the way they have been produced.

Complete harmonisation of social and environmental standards is neither practical nor desirable, and is not sought in any existing trade agreements. But this report will make the case that weak social and environmental regulations are not a source of legitimate comparative advantage, but an unacceptable form of exploitation. World trade rules should therefore be reformed to protect people's basic rights, and to promote sustainable development.

Many citizens' groups and NGOs would argue, however, that the WTO has no competence in these areas, and that its reputation for secrecy and exclusivity, together with its distance from the UN system, and dominance by Northern governments and TNCs, make it an inappropriate forum in which to make decisions on social and environmental issues.

These are legitimate concerns. In the consideration and analysis of the social and environmental regulation of international trade which is developed in the next two chapters, and in the recommendations which follow in chapter four, it is not envisaged that the WTO itself would play the lead role in either area. The ILO is clearly the most appropriate body to make judgements over labour standards and, in the absence of a comparable environmental body, it is proposed that an Intergovernmental Panel on Trade and Sustainable Development be established to develop standards for environmental protection. The WTO itself is in urgent need of reform to make it more transparent, democratic, and accountable, and a range of proposals are made in chapter four to work towards this.

CHAPTER TWO:
INTERNATIONAL TRADE AND LABOUR STANDARDS

The garments industry in Bangladesh

On the night of 21 November 1995, 30 armed men smashed their way into the offices of the Bangladesh Independent Garment Workers' Union (BIGU). They held the union's lawyer, Fawzia Karim Feroze, at gun-point, ripped off her sari, soaked her in petrol, and tried to set her on fire. They threatened to shoot anyone who spoke out. Then they went on the rampage, firing into the air, destroying files, breaking windows, and even tried to set fire to the whole building.[23]

This is not the first time that the BIGU has been a target of attacks. Founded in December 1994, it campaigns for better conditions for women in the garments industry, and has had some notable successes. It is clearly seen as a threat by some in the industry, who fear that their competitiveness and profits are at stake.

In this chapter we will focus on the competitive pressures facing the garments industry in Bangladesh, and on measures that can be taken to improve labour standards in the factories. The process of 'competitive impoverishment' is not inevitable but depends on the policies and actions of retailers, governments, and international bodies. Together with workers' and consumers' organisations, Oxfam is working to ensure that these bodies uphold and respect the internationally agreed rights of all people to a decent and secure livelihood. The roles of consumer pressure, codes of conduct, ILO Conventions, and the WTO are explored, and the case is made, subject to certain conditions outlined later in this book, for the introduction of a social clause which would link membership of the WTO to respect for certain minimum labour standards.

From a modest beginning as a non-traditional export sector, which earned £4 million in 1981, the garments industry in Bangladesh has witnessed a phenomenal growth. In 1994-95, export earnings from this sector reached £1.2 billion, making it the largest export earner for Bangladesh, contributing 57 per cent of total foreign exchange earnings. Garment making has also become the largest source of employment generation. Over 1.2 million people, 90 per cent of them women, work in the garment sector and its ancillary industries.[24] Today Bangladesh has some 2,400 garment factories, mostly located in and around the capital Dhaka, and the southern port cities of Chittagong and Khulna. Much of their production is destined for the US and Europe.[25]

Several factors currently threaten the industry, however, suggesting that its success is built on insecure foundations. As the table below demonstrates, output per worker is very low. The bulk of production is also low value-added; the finished garments are intended for the lower end of the market, so the profit margins are small, leaving Bangladesh in a highly vulnerable position as markets become more competitive.[26]

Table 1 *Comparative output per worker in the garments industry*

Country	Person minutes per basic shirt
USA	14.00
Hongkong	19.75
South Korea	20.75
Sri Lanka	24.00
Bangladesh	25.00

Bangladesh is also dependent on external sources for its textiles. Just 4 per cent of the 2.25 billion yards of fabric required by the industry in 1994 could be supplied by local textile manufacturers; the rest was imported, mainly from Asian textile producers. Not only does this lack of backward linkages in the economy reduce the profits which Bangladesh can make – one estimate suggests that only 30 per cent of the total value of exported garments remains in the country, with the other 70 per cent paid out for imported fabrics – it also adds considerably to the turn-around time on production.[27] One exporter recently observed,

Orders currently take about four months, when what we really need to achieve is a 30-day turn-around on orders. We have to import all our fabrics so we need credit letters, we have import bills and money is held up longer. The only survival for us is the development of a textiles industry here in Bangladesh.[28]

It will be extremely difficult for Bangladesh to make this significant new step without a sure, steady future for its markets. The phasing-out of the Multi-Fibre Arrangement (MFA) is making this both more urgent – because the industry will have to become more competitive – and more difficult – because its future markets are becoming less secure.[29] For while the effect of the MFA on developing countries as a whole has undoubtedly been a negative one, some countries, including Bangladesh, have paradoxically benefited from it in some ways. One of the factors behind the garments boom in Bangladesh was the search for ways through the barrier of the MFA by firms from the Asian NICs (newly industrialised countries). In the early 1980s the industrialised countries placed relatively few quota restrictions on clothing exports from Bangladesh, making it an attractive location for East Asian firms that had used up all the export possibilities allowed to them in their home country under the MFA. A study of foreign direct investments in Bangladesh in the late 1980s found that over 40 per cent of the companies involved were from the Asian NICS; and 70 per cent of the investments were in the clothing industry.[30]

While the MFA gave Bangladesh some degree of competitive advantage in terms of market access over established competitors such as China, Hong Kong, and India, its phase-out will mean Bangladesh will have to compete with its giant neighbours under a free market regime.[31] Since Bangladesh cannot currently compete in terms of productivity nor, any longer, in terms of market access, there is a significant danger that it will resort to exploiting still further the final factor of its competitive advantage: low labour costs.

A large pool of cheap labour has been critical to the industry's success. As one prominent exporter put it, 'Only a cheaper price will make the orders come to me.'[32]

Table 2 *Comparative average hourly wages in the garments industry*[33]

Country	Hourly wage in US$
Germany	25.00
USA	16.00
South Korea	5.00
Mexico	2.40
Poland	1.40
Sri Lanka	0.45
China	0.35
India	0.35
Nepal	0.30
Bangladesh	0.15

However, new competitors are already appearing in the region, notably Vietnam, which has a skilled labour force of over 130,000 people in the garments industry and had, in 1992, an installed production capacity of about 110 million garments per year. Its labour is one of the cheapest in the world. Vietnam is actively exploring new export markets and many major European buyers have already set up there. Cambodia and Laos may also eventually become suppliers of garments in international markets. Some evidence suggests that business is already beginning to leave Bangladesh for these new production sites.[34] If Bangladesh lowers the standards of working conditions in its factories still further in order to remain competitive, the prospects for its workers will be grim.

Case study

Selina Akhter became a garment worker when she was just 14 years old. Both her parents had died and Selina was dependent on her uncle's family. 'I had to earn my keep and there seemed to be no other job for me.' She started as a 'helper', and very soon became a machine operator, earning 450 taka per month as her basic wage. She has worked in different garment factories ever since; now, 11 years later, she is still a machine operator, and her salary is only 1,400 taka despite her long experience.[35]

She currently works in a small factory in the Mirpur district of Dhaka. The hours are long and gruelling. Most of the factories she has worked in do not observe the eight-hourly duty rule:

We are usually given targets for a day which are set so high that it's impossible to fulfil them in eight hours. Say they ask us to finish 2,000 pieces in one shift. Usually 10-12 hours go in meeting the target. On top of it, we have frequent night duties, especially before the shipment.

This factory and many others either postpone paying overtime or avoid it altogether. Selina always has three months' overtime pay pending; sometimes she doesn't get it at all:

If you are absent for one day, the management deduct three days' wages from your income. You could complain to your supervisor, line chief, or even to the production manager. But don't expect any redress.

One of the main reasons why workers like Selina keep changing jobs is that the factories simply dismiss them: sometimes because it's a lean period; sometimes if a worker is seen as a troublemaker by speaking out and protesting; or sometimes if a worker falls ill. They are powerless against such arbitrary treatment. As Selina says, she had to submit a written application along with her photograph to each of the factories where she has worked, but in only one factory was she ever given any appointment document.

The impact on women

The vast majority of women working in the factories are young women like Selina, who have migrated from rural areas to the cities in search of employment.[36] For them, working in garment factories represents a release from more manual, poorly paid, or unpaid forms of rural employment. Because of the destitution they have left behind, even an exploitative industrial environment provides a means of freedom from the miseries of oppression, hunger, and poverty.[37]

It has also enabled many women to enjoy a new-found independence and status. Their lives have changed since they joined the garment factories. Most of them used to stay inside their homes, not venturing outside by themselves. Now they are no longer afraid to move freely, and are more likely to have a decision-making role in the family.[38] They are also less dependent on their parents, and more able to resist a forced early marriage. The continued success of the garments industry is therefore critical to these young women.

It is important, at the same time, not to overestimate the effects of this revolution. While employment in the garment factories might improve the terms on which young women are able to negotiate the social relations that subordinate them, the underlying structures of gender inequality do not automatically disappear in that process, any more than they did in nineteenth-century Lancashire when thousands of young women went to work in textile mills.[39]

Nevertheless, women are becoming more aware of their rights, and gradually, in spite of the double burden of employment and family responsibilities, and despite the male-dominated union hierarchies, they are beginning to assert them.

Union demands

On 26 July 1995 the front page of one of Dhaka's English daily newspapers, the *Financial Express*, was emblazoned with the headline: 'Garment workers demand minimum pay, 8hr work day'. At a press conference the previous day, General Secretary of the National Garment Workers' Federation, Amirul Huq Amin, accused the garments industry of conditions amounting to 'modern slavery', and launched the start of a sustained campaign of rallies and protests to draw attention to working conditions. Women have been marching in the streets to demand the right to one day off a week, which they regard as a 'legal and human right', the right to payment of the minimum wage, and a standard working week of 48 hours. Garment workers have to work 14-16 hours a day, and are rarely paid the amount to which they are legally entitled. 'We have to work from 8am to 10-11pm seven days a week', claimed Amin. 'We have no holiday.'

There has been no shortage of reports into the grim working conditions in many of the factories.[40] The neglect of health and safety issues was most recently and graphically brought to people's attention by a fire at Lusaka Garments Factory in the Ibrahimpur area of Dhaka in August 1995, which left nine young people dead. The seven-storey building housed three garment factories, and it is thought that most of those who died were killed in the stampede down the narrow staircase.

This sort of tragedy is all too frequent in Bangladesh's garment factories. In the last five years, at least 50 workers have lost their lives in similar fires. The worst was at Saraka Garments in the Mirpur area of Dhaka five years ago, when 30 people died. Most factories ignore the legal requirement to have fire-fighting equipment in the building, and some have locked gates during working hours, making it impossible for workers to escape.

In theory, the working day in factories is from 8am to 4.30pm with half an hour for lunch, but many workers often have to work until 8pm, or even later if there are deadlines to meet. Overtime is frequently paid late, and sometimes not at all. Often workers work seven days a week, without the statutory day off per week. Eid and holiday bonuses, to which workers are traditionally entitled, are frequently not given. Some factories penalise workers for being late by docking their salary; if a worker is absent for three consecutive days (e.g. due to sickness), she can be fired.

The Bangladesh Factory Act of 1965 is routinely ignored. It stipulates, for example, that workers are entitled to a weekly holiday, and that no worker should be allowed to work more than 60 hours per week or 10 hours per day. Bangladesh Labour Law 19 (a) states that a worker has to be given three months' notice before termination of employment: this is frequently ignored, and garment workers are liable to be fired on the spot. The government has declared that the minimum wage for garment workers should be Tk. 950 per month, but few employers abide by that rule. Apprentices often get just Tk. 300 per month.

Incidents of sexual harassment of women frequently take place, both by managers within the factories, and by local youths when the women are walking to and from work. This explains why safe transport home after late shifts is one of the women's main demands. The demands presented by the National Garment Workers' Federation to the Government last year also include:

- implementation of minimum wage regulation
- payment of salary and overtime within the first week of the month
- provision of a medical doctor and health facilities
- provision of clean toilets, safe drinking water, canteen and recreation room
- Eid and other holiday bonuses
- three months' paid leave for childbirth
- no work during government holidays.

Although Bangladesh has ratified ILO Conventions 87 and 98 on freedom of association and the right to organise, and in spite of the fact that their own laws in principle also guarantee union rights, most managers do not allow unions to operate in their factories. Many workers are therefore afraid to join unions in case they lose their jobs.

The industry also has a vast chain of sub-contracting units, some no larger than the front room of a house. If they have fewer than 25 employees, they are not covered by the Factories Act, and conditions are even harder to monitor. Two years ago when a workers' strike brought production to a halt in a garment factory in Bangladesh, instead of conceding the demand for a festival holiday, the management merely sub-contracted their orders. Export schedules were thus maintained but the workers lost their jobs.[41]

More recently, the whole workforce at Titas Apparels in Dhaka were fired, after union members went on strike. Titas Apparels Garment Workers' and Employees' Union was formally registered in June 1995. Later in the year, it presented a list of demands to the factory management, covering payment of the minimum wage, and full and prompt payment of overtime, legal holidays, paid sick leave, and compensation in case of accidents. They also requested an end to management intimidation of union members. They received no response, and took the issue to the government's Labour Department. When the employers continued to fail to respond, the union called a strike. The strike began on 27 December. On 30 December, the owners closed the factory, sacking all 350 workers.[42]

Added to the ongoing problems of low productivity, and lack of backward linkages in the economy, the industry in Bangladesh is currently facing an additional burden because of the extremely serious political crisis, which is resulting in lost orders and forcing factory closures. This has been gathering momentum over the past 18 months but now, following the controversial parliamentary elections of 15 February 1996, which were boycotted by the main opposition party, political disturbances, civil unrest, and protracted 'hartels', or enforced mass strikes of all public services and private enterprises, have dramatically increased. Overseas buyers are understandably becoming reluctant to place orders with Bangladeshi firms since they now risk significant delays in production deadlines.

Bangladesh offers an interesting illustration of the links between trade liberalisation and labour standards because of the pressure it is currently experiencing to improve its competitive advantage, particularly as a result of the phasing out of the MFA. However, the conditions in Bangladeshi factories are currently no worse than in many others in Asia and Latin America. Over the past 20 years there has been a phenomenal increase in the number of companies setting up in the Free Trade Zones of the Dominican Republic, for example, many of them making textiles and clothing.[43] Around three-quarters of the workers are women, and the conditions they complain of are similar to those in

Bangladesh: long hours without adequate breaks, forced overtime, intimidation and harassment at work, poor salary (often below the minimum wage), and arbitrary dismissal.

Measures to improve conditions

There is clearly an important role for government to play in improving factory conditions, both in enacting legislation, and in ensuring compliance with it. However, in an increasingly global economy, it is becoming even more difficult for governments significantly to improve conditions on their own: international measures are therefore also needed, and a number have been proposed. A brief examination of one of them, the Harkin Bill, will serve to emphasise the importance of ensuring that minimum standards are *appropriate and equitable* as well as feasible.

In 1993 US Senator Tom Harkin put down a Bill in the US Congress which would prohibit the import into the US of goods made with child labour. The immediate effect of the Bill in Bangladesh was dramatic: as many as 40,000 children were promptly thrown out of the factories, and many more have been forced to leave since. Studies by UNICEF and others indicate that many of them were driven to find work in more dangerous occupations under even harsher conditions: breaking bricks all day in the glaring sun, for example, or prostitution. In 1995 Harkin reintroduced the Bill (The Child Labour Deterrence Act). Although it has still to be passed, the pressure it created was enough to push the BGMEA (Bangladesh Garment Manufacturers' and Exporters' Association) to sign a Memorandum of Understanding (MOU) with the ILO and UNICEF which would bring an end to child labour in the garment factories. While in principle this is, of course, to be welcomed, in Oxfam's view, based on our experience in Bangladesh, the MOU, which was finally signed on 4 July 1995, has some serious flaws.

For example, evidence suggests that many thousands of children were sacked – often without receiving the pay owing to them – before the terms of the MOU came into effect.[44] This enabled factory owners to avoid making provision for the children to receive the schooling which the MOU envisages for them. Many of these children are likely now to be in even more exploitative employment.

There is no birth registration in Bangladesh, and therefore no way of verifying a person's age. Furthermore, poor nutrition can result in late development. A child who looks ten years old could easily be 14 or older. The operation of the MOU will be based on a 'rapid assessment' of children's ages, which will inevitably be very subjective. The 'expert's' opinion will presumably take precedence over the child's claim, thereby seriously undermining his or her rights.

Moreover, by focusing on the child labour issue alone, the MOU does nothing to tackle the much broader issue of factory conditions in general. It would be more effective to press for better overall standards, which would include shorter shifts for children, together with education provision *in the factories themselves* (where it could be more effectively monitored), and thereby help to eradicate the poverty which is the root cause of this kind of child labour. Introducing measures to ban child labour almost overnight, without adequate provision for and investment in education and poverty alleviation (a responsibility of both national governments and the international community), is likely to be counter-productive, and simply shift it to a less visible (and more exploitative) part of the economy. Although the MOU contains a commitment to paying children 300 taka per month as an incentive towards undergoing schooling, unions and some NGOs are concerned that this will not be sufficient: many children could earn more than that by working, and for some, maximising the amount they can earn now is critical to their survival.[45]

That ample scope exists for introducing better conditions is illustrated by the example of the Bantai factory in Dhaka, one of a small number of factories which are beginning to address social issues. Its manager, Saidur Rahman, has already implemented a number of schemes which both benefit its workforce and, he claims, make good economic sense. A health-care scheme, creche and school are offered, for example. A doctor linked to Dhaka

Community Hospital (which is supported by Oxfam) runs a weekly surgery in this factory, and in several others: those paying into the health scheme are also entitled to attend the hospital and have full health cover for their immediate families. Although the working day is very long (a basic 10-12-hour day), overtime semi-compulsory at busy times, and even here no unions are set up, the pay is good, and workers get regular breaks. Rahman is convinced his management style is both profitable and replicable:

It's good economics, as well as good conditions. Contented people work well and stay with the factory over time – it's good for business.

Codes of conduct

There are a number of ways in which pressure to improve conditions in the factories can be generated. These range from consumer pressure in importing countries, to national and international pressure on governments and business to ensure the ratification and implementation of relevant ILO Conventions, and finally to international regulation of labour standards via trade and investment agreements. They are largely complementary strategies, and Oxfam is pursuing them all in its international campaign to improve the situation of garment workers worldwide.[46]

At first it may seem that the garments industry is not an easy area for consumers to exert their influence on. Very few manufacturers sell direct to the public. The long manufacturing chain, often involving a number of different companies and sub-contractors, and covering several different countries, can make it difficult for consumers to link brands to manufacturers. On the other hand, retailers are in a unique position: since they produce designs and then take patterns around to manufacturers until they find the best deal, it is ultimately they who are responsible for what is produced, where, for what wages, and under what conditions. In the UK, just seven retailers account for nearly half of the total market value in the sector, and dominate total sales. High-street clothing retailers, therefore, can be the primary link between consumers and the clothing manufacturers, and our main assurances or knowledge about conditions of manufacture should be able to come through them.

One tool which can be used to encourage retailers and manufacturers to improve standards across an industry is a voluntary code of conduct. Such codes are being developed by a wide range of NGOs, consumer groups, unions, and workers' organisations, and are having some success. The European-wide Clean Clothes Campaign, for example, was launched in 1990, and includes provision for a 'window trademark' which would be awarded to those retailers who make significant progress towards certain standards. The mark would be displayed, so that retailers could advertise themselves as sellers of 'clean clothes', and their ongoing behaviour would be regularly and independently monitored.[47]

Oxfam is currently developing its own code, or 'Challenge to Retailers', to use in its campaign to encourage improvements for workers in the garments industry. It is based on ILO Conventions, and starts from the principle that retailers and manufacturers should accept responsibility for the social and employment conditions under which their products are made, throughout the subcontracting chain, whether at home or overseas.

Representatives of workers should be involved in the interpretation of the Conventions, and in the development of more detailed standards which are appropriate to the local situation, and in the verification process. All the provisions of the code should apply equally to temporary and permanent workers, and to homeworkers. It should be translated into local languages and prominently displayed in the place of work.

The Code should set some fundamental principles as aims to which companies should direct their efforts. Companies are to be judged by their progress towards implementation of these goals, rather than their immediate achievement. This will enable companies to enter into serious dialogue with their suppliers in a strategy of positive engagement, rather than taking the simpler route of immediately withdrawing their business. On the issue of child labour, for example, there are a range of measures which could be taken to improve conditions for children: they include offering part-time schooling within the factories, training, and protection from hazardous employment, as well as better wages for adults (so that they will be less likely to need to send children out to work). However, if a particular supplier is unwilling to make reasonable progress towards meeting these standards, particularly where other suppliers are ready to do so, this should be a major factor in deciding whether a trading relationship should continue.

Monitoring is vital to the success of any code, and it should include visits to factories, and discussions with representatives of the workers. There should be independent auditing of the results.

Oxfam's 'Challenge to Retailers' covers the following issues:[48]

- freedom of association and collective bargaining
- equality of treatment
- wages
- working hours
- health and safety
- security of employment
- social security
- employment of children
- forced labour.

The weakness of any code of conduct, however, remains its voluntary nature, and the constant danger that good practice in one factory will be undercut by bad practice in another. A code of conduct can be a useful and effective instrument, but ultimately it needs to be supported by government legislation backed by a core of internationally agreed binding labour rights.[49]

The role of the ILO

Currently, the most significant multilateral mechanism for improving labour standards remains the ILO, now a specialist agency of the United Nations. In its commentary on Article 22 of the International Convention on Civil and Political Rights, the UN Human Rights Committee specifies that governments must ensure that their laws conform to the guarantees set out by the ILO's 1948 Convention. This reflects the ILO's importance in monitoring the employment laws of individual countries and measuring them against international human rights standards. There are now 170 countries who are members of the ILO, each entitled to send four delegates to its annual decision-making conference: two government representatives, one representative of employers, and one of employees, reflecting the ILO's unique tripartite structure.

Since it was founded in 1919, the ILO has adopted over 174 Conventions covering a wide range of labour standards. The ILO has no legal powers of enforcement, relying instead on persuasion, peer pressure, and the power of public opinion.

Each member state is required periodically to submit for examination a report relating to its progress in implementing those conventions which it has ratified. There are also a number of formal complaints mechanisms. Under the *representation procedure* employers' or workers' representatives can submit allegations of a failure by a member country to adopt satisfactory measures. If accepted by the ILO, an ad hoc tripartite body is set up to consider the case and make recommendations. Since 1980 there have been 33 representation procedures.

In a more formal *complaints procedure*, a complaint may be filed by any member state if it is not satisfied that any other member is securing the effective observance of any Convention which both have ratified. Complaints may also be initiated by the Governing Body of the ILO either on its own motion or on receipt of information from a delegate (employer or worker) to the ILO Conference. This is then considered by a Commission of Inquiry, which makes recommendations, which are published and may be challenged before the International Court of Justice, whose ruling is final. If a member country fails to effect the recommendations or ruling, the ILO Governing Body may recommend any measure it deems necessary. In practice, no sanctions of any consequence have ever been applied in any of the 24 complaints procedures carried out since the founding of the ILO.

There is an exceptional procedure in the case of freedom of association, in which a specially established tripartite Committee on Freedom of Association examines complaints concerning the denial of this freedom, regardless of whether or not the countries concerned have ratified the relevant Conventions. Complaints are considered three times a year, and the Committee can reach either interim or definitive conclusions, or it can decide that a case does not warrant further investigation. The pressure it can exert has resulted in some notable successes: among the most dramatic have been the withdrawal of the death penalty from trade unionists, freeing of trade unionists from prison, the reinstatement of trade union leaders and workers dismissed following strikes, and the reversal of decisions to dissolve trade unions.[50] Nearly 1,900 cases have been examined under this procedure, and the studies of the Committee have developed a significant body of precedent on the interpretation of the ILO provisions in this field.

With the exception of this Committee, however, governments can only be subject to ILO examination with respect to conventions which they have decided freely to ratify, and the findings of the ILO supervisory bodies are not always acted upon.

Reform of the ILO

Although the ILO now has over 170 members and covers 98 per cent of the world's population, there has been a fall in ratifications in recent years, and a growing sense that its processes, based on moral persuasion or 'the mobilisation of shame' alone, are no longer sufficient.

In particular, the voluntary nature of the Conventions prevents them from playing a full part in the regulation of international trade, while the focus of the ILO standards themselves is exclusively on national governments. With the new challenges of economic globalisation, even governments of the most powerful states are finding it hard to pursue autonomous economic and social policies effectively, when hugely powerful TNCs can shift production sites across borders or oceans to cut costs and maximise profits.

During the review of the ILO's activities at its seventy-fifth anniversary in 1994, its Director General himself emphasised the need for the ILO to become more involved in the discussions on the social dimensions of trade liberalisation, warning that it would be difficult for the organisation most concerned with labour standards to 'stand aloof from the debate without the risk of being relegated to the sidelines'.[51]

Enhanced Freedom of Association Procedure

The Workers' Group of the ILO Governing Body, together with the International Confederation of Free Trade Unions (ICFTU), have long argued the same position, and pointed to the discrepancy between principles and practice with respect to a number of widely ratified Conventions relating to basic human rights. The most fundamental standards relating to freedom of association, discrimination, and forced labour are frequently flouted, even by countries which have ratified the Conventions; while a number of countries, in their failure to ratify these instruments, are evading the basic obligations of their membership of the ILO.

More specifically, the unions have proposed that the logic which underpinned the establishment of the Committee on Freedom of Association should be more widely applied through the establishment of mechanisms through which complaints can be presented against governments for violations of the principles set out in the Conventions on discrimination and on forced labour. As with the Committee on Freedom of Association, governments would be subject to these mechanisms regardless of whether they have ratified the instruments in question.

Recently, some more detailed recommendations on possible implementation procedures for the extension of the Freedom of Association mechanism have been put forward.[52] It seems unlikely that the existing Committee will have its remit extended. Alternatives would be one new committee to deal with forced labour and discrimination, or two separate ones. The specific content of such a procedure has yet to be agreed, and discussions within the ILO are continuing, but it is clear that such a procedure could make an important contribution towards improving labour standards by raising the profile of the whole body of core human rights conventions.

But while such reform would be a welcome step towards strengthening the ILO's provisions, and enabling it to play a more significant role in trade issues, the problem of a lack of enforcement measures would remain. To have a real impact, these new, standards-setting structures should, as the Workers' Group of the ILO's Governing Body clearly states, be developed simultaneously with a renewed initiative for a social clause to be included in the WTO Agreement.

The case for a social clause

What is it?

A social clause in an international trade agreement is intended to improve labour conditions in exporting countries by allowing sanctions to be taken against exporters who fail to observe minimum standards. A typical social clause of this kind makes it possible to restrict or halt the importation or preferential importation of products originating in countries, industries, or firms where labour conditions do not meet certain minimum standards. Producers who do not comply with the minimum requirements must choose between a change in working conditions or the risk of being confronted with increased trade barriers in their export markets.[53]

Clearly the major impact of a social clause will be limited to the export sector, although some evidence suggests that there can be a 'knock-on' effect by pulling up standards in other sectors.[54] It should not be seen as a panacea for all labour problems, but as a tool which can be used to support basic rights and prevent the worst excesses of labour exploitation for a significant number of people.[55]

What would it comprise?

Much of the controversy around the concept of a social clause results from misunderstandings about which Conventions it would include. Many opponents of the idea fear that it is little more than a smokescreen for protectionism, and that the aim of labour unions in the developed economies is to destroy the South's comparative advantage in lower wage costs by imposing minimum wages and specific conditions of work which are currently inappropriate in many developing countries. This is not the intention. Along with international trade unions and others, Oxfam believes that it is possible to distinguish between different kinds of labour standards: those aimed at ensuring core standards or fundamental human rights, and those related to more detailed, often technical and industry-specific, conditions.

The kind of social clause envisaged would be based on a package of basic human rights (set out below) which should and can exist in any country irrespective of its current state of development. These are enabling rights, designed to guarantee the possibility (but not the content) of social progress, and they therefore make no attempt to equalise costs or to prescribe minimum wage levels. Oxfam believes that consideration should be given to including the following ILO Conventions in a social clause:

> No.87: Freedom of Association and Protection of the Right to Organise
>
> No.98: Right to Organise and Collective Bargaining
>
> No.100: Right to Equal Remuneration for Men and Women Workers
>
> No.111: Freedom from Discrimination
>
> Nos.29 and 105: The Abolition of Forced Labour.

In the first instance, however, negotiations on a social clause should be limited to the incorporation of Conventions 87 and 98 only. This is partly because they are the most fundamental ones, and to some extent, adherence to them is a prerequisite for achieving any other standards. The trade union rights enshrined in these two Conventions give workers the right to negotiate with governments and employers' organisations for whatever wage levels and conditions they consider appropriate under the prevailing socio-economic conditions. Additionally, the authority of the ILO itself depends on its unique tripartite structure, which in turn depends on the freedom of workers and employers freely to associate. To that extent, membership of the ILO is often interpreted as automatically bringing with it the obligation to recognise the freedom of association and right to organise.

These rights are also the most directly trade-related, and little further research and analysis would be required to determine how they might be incorporated into a social clause. The monitoring machinery to a large extent already exists, in the form of the ILO's Freedom of Association Committee, and a significant amount of legal knowledge and experience has been developed on the interpretation of the ILO provisions in this field.

Should a social clause cover child labour?

Many proposals for a social clause, including those from the ICFTU, also include Convention 138 on the minimum age of admission to employment. Oxfam is committed to the eradication of all forms of exploitative child labour, and believes that its most extreme forms (child servitude and bonded labour, for example) should be abolished. The ILO Workers' Group shares this position.

The exploitation of children's labour is an extremely deep-rooted problem, with many causes and no simple solutions. Millions of children suffer as a result of working too young, for too many hours, and in hazardous conditions, and by the time they reach adulthood, they are often damaged physically and mentally, and have lost the opportunity for an education which could have opened up the possibility of a better future.[56]

There are many different kinds of work that are covered by the term 'child labour', however, and it is helpful to distinguish between them. There is some work that children perform that is clearly not exploitative, does not interfere with their education, and indeed is a part of growing up (helping on a family farm after school, for example). At the other extreme, bonded labour or child slavery is clearly totally unacceptable and should be abolished immediately. This could be achieved through the effective implementation of Conventions 29 and 105, or through a specially designed new convention (see below).

In between these two extremes of child work and child servitude lies a grey area of child labour, about which it is very difficult to generalise. In Oxfam's experience, the most significant cause of child labour is the widespread poverty, unemployment, and low wages which force families into a situation where children have to earn an income in order for the family to survive. In many cases, the costs of schooling would in any case be prohibitive (even when schooling is theoretically 'free', parents often have to pay for uniforms and books), or schools simply do not exist in the vicinity. In the longer term, therefore, much of the solution lies in urgently tackling these underlying economic, political, and social factors, and both national governments and the international community should take greater responsibility for funding programmes to address them.

In the meantime, there is a significant danger that the inclusion of Convention 138 into a social clause could lead to a blanket ban on all child labour which, in the absence of adequate investment in poverty alleviation and education, could be counter-productive. Children could simply be thrown out of the factories, and face a life of destitution; or they could be forced into even more exploitative employment in a domestic industry, or in the informal sector where any form of monitoring or control becomes impossible. On the other hand, it is sometimes argued that child labour is often found in areas of high adult unemployment, and that if a child were banned from working, an adult family member could replace him or her, resulting in no reduction in family income. If children were effectively banned from working, this would improve the bargaining position of adults. These are valid arguments, and serve to underline the danger of generalisations, and the need to address the issue on a case-by-case basis.

The social clause proposed above would be a step towards creating the conditions necessary to abolish child labour in the longer term, by giving workers the right to negotiate better terms and conditions with their employers, so that the family would no longer be dependent on child labour for its survival. Children currently in the workplace would also benefit from the better conditions which could be negotiated: many unions include among their demands that children should be fairly paid, properly protected (undertaking only light work, for example), and trained. It is also likely that, where unions are strong, they will usually resist the hiring of children at wage rates which undermine those of adult workers.

First reports of current discussions within the ILO about a new Convention which would cover the 'most intolerable' forms of child labour sound interesting. The definition of 'most intolerable' has still to be agreed, but if it includes the most hazardous forms of labour, child servitude, bonded labour, the sex industry, and labour of the very young, then it may indeed be an appropriate Convention to consider including within a social clause, since it would cover those areas of most extreme exploitation for which there can be no economic, political, or social justification.[57]

How would a social clause help?

The political sensitivities surrounding the incorporation of a social clause into the Uruguay Round treaty are generated by very real concerns. Many Southern governments and NGOs are justifiably suspicious of the motivation behind the proposal, fearing that it is yet another way of keeping out cheaper Southern goods from Northern markets. The unequivocal verdict of Martin Khor, Director of the influential Southern NGO, Third World Network, is that:[58]

The attempt...to introduce 'labour standards' and 'workers' rights' as issues for the WTO to take up is quite clearly prompted not by feelings of goodwill towards Third World workers, but by protectionist attempts to prevent the transfer of jobs from North to South.

Undoubtedly there is a strong political current of anti-trade protectionism in current Northern politics (we need look no further than the political agenda of Le Pen in France, or Pat Buchanan in the US), and we are therefore presented with very difficult political decisions. Ultimately, however, the choice before us is this: do we want an international trading system which throws workers into competition with one another for jobs, leading to a downward spiral of working conditions as each country undercuts the others; or a win/win scenario, whereby an international floor of minimum labour standards protects all workers from unacceptable levels of exploitation? This would *not* mean removing the South's current competitive advantage in low costs: it *would* mean giving workers some minimum level of protection.

The aim of a social clause is to prevent the erosion of good working practices by competition from bad ones, and to promote basic rights where they are not already respected. There is both a moral and an economic case in its favour. The moral argument is simply put as the need to safeguard certain basic rights in core labour standards, which should and can be respected regardless of a nation's level of economic development.

This has been dismissed by some as a 'Northern' perception of fundamental rights, which is a 'values-related argument for suspending another country's trading rights'.[59] As the Workers' Group of the ILO Governing Body observes, however, the vast majority of WTO members are already signatories to these core human rights (all of those envisaged as part of a basic rights package have over 100 signatories: as at April 1995, Convention 87 had received 113 ratifications; Convention 98, 125 ratifications).

They also point out that two-thirds of their own membership is from outside the developed world and thus clearly have no protectionist intent. These measures do not therefore represent a coercive set of new conditions, but rather agreement on the acceptable standards for engagement in the multilateral trading system. If international trade is to be conducted under the auspices of an equitable, open, and rules-based system, then governments must be prepared to accept a reciprocal obligation to enforce minimum standards.

There is also a strong social and economic case for a social clause. The preamble to the WTO refers to the objective of raising standards of living: one rationale for a social clause is to realise this objective which has not, and can never be, achieved through a 'trickle down' effect from trade liberalisation alone. A social clause would help to ensure that trade supports rather than undermines workers' rights, and would enable the benefits of trade to feed through to workers. For workers in countries where the rights to freedom of association, to organise, and to collective bargaining are absent or restricted, it would offer an international lever to pressurise their own national governments and employers, and indeed it would help those governments and employers who wish to improve workers' living conditions by reducing competition from exploitative labour practices elsewhere.

It would not include setting internationally agreed minimum wage levels, to which Southern groups quite rightly object. As Martin Khor observes:

In reality low wage levels paid by ...the South may not necessarily or primarily be caused by a deliberate policy of labour exploitation...They are mainly due to the prevailing low levels of income and living standards of the general population.[60]

It follows that the question of raising incomes cannot be addressed outside of broader questions of development strategies and resource distribution. However, low income-levels cannot be a justification for the suppression of basic human rights, a trend which is accelerating. In its annual survey for 1995, the ICFTU revealed that there had been a 65 per cent increase in repressive government action against organised labour in the previous three years, spreading to 98 countries; the highest total so far.[61]

It is precisely through the exercise of the right freely to associate and organise that workers can negotiate for whatever wage levels and labour standards are considered appropriate under the prevailing socio-economic conditions in their country. Khor concludes:

The raising of 'labour standards' to approach Northern levels, or to cross beyond market parameters (when a country's general living standards are still low) may well result in more harm than good for the South (including its workers) if it results in closure of industries and thus job retrenchments.

This is undoubtedly true. But we are not proposing that Southern labour standards should approach Northern levels: what we are proposing is that there is a core of basic human rights which should be recognised by every country, without exception. Furthermore, if unions have the right to bargain collectively with employers, it is highly unlikely that they will deliberately act against their own interests by bidding up wages and conditions to the point where a factory can no longer be competitive, and has to close. Moreover, it would provide incentives to companies to adopt strategies aimed at increasing productivity through higher value-added, including investment in skills development and technology, rather than relying on cheap labour for competitive advantage.

Many groups in the South see the social clause as an attempt to prevent job losses in the North, and rightly point out that the North's unemployment crisis cannot be blamed solely on the transfer of industries to the low-cost South. Unemployment in the North has many causes, including governments' deflationary macro-economic policies, high interest rates, inadequate investment in education and training, and technological changes; although the impact of job losses to the South in certain industries has sometimes been underestimated.

But it is also true that foreign investment is integrating national economies and labour markets into an increasingly globalised system. This has profound implications because of the divergence in living standards between countries. Companies are therefore able to use the threat to move to the South to bargain down working conditions. Workers are in effect being put in competition with one another by companies who will give the jobs to those who are willing to work under the poorest conditions, and thus take jobs from those who demand better. This is happening within the developing world, as well as between North and South. Unskilled workers in the newly industrialised countries (NICs) – South Korea, Taiwan, Singapore, and Hong Kong – are losing jobs to workers in countries such as Thailand, Malaysia, and the Philippines, who in turn are now beginning to lose jobs to even cheaper labour in China, Vietnam, and Indonesia.

These forces carry with them the threat of downward pressure on social standards worldwide, as the fear of losing foreign investment or of becoming uncompetitive forces governments to even lower standards. The current debate in the European Union is a case in point: the UK Government is resisting European legislation to introduce a 48-hour limit to the working week on the grounds that: 'It is precisely because of legislation like this and stupidities like this that the EU is becoming uncompetitive and losing jobs to other parts of the world.'[62]

As the ICFTU has concluded:

It is at present all too easy for some countries to violate these rights in order to establish a competitive advantage over their neighbours and trading partners. The effect is to force other trading countries to consider reducing their own workers' rights to the same level. Thus a vicious circle of competition based on cutting labour costs can develop.[63]

The only effective way to prevent a downward spiral of conditions, therefore, is to establish an internationally agreed and regulated floor level for workers' rights below which no nation may go.

A further criticism levelled at the social clause is that it will benefit workers only in the formal sector. However, in many countries an increasing proportion of the so-called 'self-employed' informal sector workers are dependent on large formal sector companies, including TNCs, for their livelihoods. This suggests that where sub-contracting is common, there may be far more scope to raise standards in the informal sector than previously assumed, by holding the formal sector company responsible for conditions in the sub-contracting chain. In such cases, far from exacerbating inequalities between formal and informal workers, adequate labour regulation would provide marginalised groups with a tool with which to organise, and help them to achieve working conditions in line with permanent workers.[64]

Further analysis is needed on the impact of a social clause on women, the majority of whom work in the informal sector. Women are grossly under-represented in most of the fora where the debate on labour standards has been taking place – unions, governments, and international institutions – and their views have not been put forward.[65] To the extent that pay and conditions of work have generally been worse for women than for men, however, the introduction of minimum labour standards may well be of greater significance to them than to men.

Finally, a transparent, multilaterally agreed social clause would also strengthen rather than weaken the multilateral system, by containing the growth of unilateral protectionist attempts to make access to markets conditional on minimum labour standards.

How might it work?

The ICFTU has proposed that a joint WTO/ILO Advisory Body be established. This body would review periodically, or on the basis of well-justified complaints, the implementation of the core rights embodied in the social clause. This would be the particular responsibility of the ILO side of the joint advisory body, and is a role that it already plays. In the event of a country failing to satisfy the standards, the case would be studied and recommendations for action proposed. The ICFTU suggests that the ILO could provide technical assistance, and that financial support might be forthcoming for the country concerned to implement national legislation and training. After an adequate period of time for the government to take necessary action (say, two years) there would be a further report. This would make one of three findings: the government concerned had fulfilled the recommendation; progress was being made towards fulfilment; or that no attempt at progress was being made. Only in the last case would trade sanctions be considered.[66]

The Uruguay Round Agreement provides for various actions that a Contracting Party can take against the failure of another Party to meet its obligations. At least three of these have been identified which could be applicable in the case of a social clause, if new obligations were to be laid down for the Contracting Parties:[67]

To regard poor conditions as a form of subsidy: Article VI provides for the application of countervailing duties to counter the effect of dumping, where a product is sold internationally 'at less than the normal value of the product', where 'normal value' is usually defined in terms of value on the domestic market. While it may be impossible to define, on an objective and universal basis, the 'normal' level of social protection, in a similar way to 'normal value' in the case of dumping, the analogy is valid, since abnormally low conditions can also distort competition. Because the liberalisation of trade is based on the freedom to negotiate and contract, it would be logical to consider that the only conditions which may be held to be 'normal' are those which are *freely* established on the labour market between supply and demand. (In practice, the notion of 'freely established' conditions will always be a difficult one because of the imbalance of power between capital and labour; but an approximate interpretation can be made.)

Poor working conditions could also be regarded as a form of subsidy, within the meaning of Article XVI of the GATT. This presupposes that they are *artificially* maintained at a low level by the will or action of the Contracting Party. This is obviously difficult to prove, but denial of the right of freedom of association by a Contracting Party may legitimately give rise to concerns that it is endeavouring to maintain working conditions at an abnormally low level.

Both these Articles allow for the application of countervailing duties, but these can only take the form of increased tariffs, equivalent to the alleged subsidy, on the import of a product manufactured in conditions contrary to the obligations undertaken by the other Contracting Party.

To regard poor conditions as a threat to life or health: A second option, supported by the European Parliament among others, would extend the general exceptions provided for by Article XX. This provision allows any Contracting Party to adopt measures restricting trade in order to protect human or animal life or health, as well as restricting the products of prison labour. The list could be extended to include certain fundamental workers' rights.

Article XX further authorises Contracting Parties to adopt restrictive measures 'in pursuance of obligations under any intergovernmental commodity agreement which conforms to criteria submitted to the Contracting Parties'. If this clause were extended appropriately, it would make it possible to subject any trade restriction measures to conditions laid down within the framework of a multilateral agreement (such as a specially agreed package of ILO Conventions) rather than to the interests of each Contracting Party. It would also have the advantage of allowing the Contracting Parties bound by the agreement in question to apply these restrictions to Parties who are not bound by it, on condition that they do not use it as a means of discrimination or disguised protectionism.

To regard poor conditions as a neglect of obligations under the Agreement: There is a third option, based on Article XXIII, which lays down much more general provisions to address significant failures to meet obligations under the Agreement. If a new provision were to be incorporated into the WTO framework which binds members to respect specific ILO Conventions, this route could be pursued. It has the advantage of greater flexibility: rather than providing for the imposition of countervailing duties, this provision allows for a system of 'representations' which may lead to consultations with any 'appropriate intergovernmental organisation' – in this case, the ILO. But it also allows for one or more of the Contracting Parties to suspend the application of any concession resulting from the Agreement.[68]

There would be significant advantages in having violations assessed under the ILO's procedures. The formal finding that a violation has taken place could only result from following the complaints procedure laid down in Article 26 of the ILO Constitution; and only after exhausting the means provided for in that Constitution (including, where appropriate, recourse to the International Court of Justice), would it be possible to consider taking any further action. This would significantly reduce the potential for abuse. Furthermore, the complaints procedure can be set in motion by a non-governmental delegate to the ILO Conference, a more accountable mechanism than exists under the purely intergovernmental framework of the WTO.

All of these possible routes require further analysis and investigation. However, they do demonstrate that it would be technically possible to insert a social clause into the existing WTO Agreement, and provide for its enforcement.

Lessons from other trade agreements

The NAFTA Side Agreement on Labour

The North American Agreement on Labour Cooperation (NAALC) at first appears highly relevant for the discussion of the multilateral social clause since it is an agreement with a strong North-South dimension to it, and includes the possibility – albeit remote – for sanctions to be taken. However, advocacy by trinational coalitions of labour and other organisations in the US, Mexico, and Canada failed in their attempt to introduce common minimum labour standards. As a result, the NAALC is primarily concerned with enforcing domestic legislation and does not introduce any new labour rights. Instead, each country is to enforce its own labour laws: the main complaint about Mexican labour laws is not that they do not exist – Mexico has ratified considerably more ILO Conventions than the United States – but that the laws are not effectively enforced. This formula, then, rejected international standards and international enforcement structures.

A further concession became necessary after Mexican negotiators refused to allow any enforceable measures related to freedom of association or collective bargaining. Instead, a three-tier set of 'labour principles' was agreed upon. The first group, 'industrial relations' (i.e. freedom of association, collective bargaining and the right to strike) could be subject only to discussion. The second group, 'technical labour standards', including prohibition of forced labour, minimum employment standards, discrimination, and protection of migrant workers, could be subject to advisory rulings by a panel of experts. Only in respect of the third group, covering child labour, minimum wage, and health and safety, can punitive actions – primarily fines – be taken up for uncorrected violations.

Moreover, the National Administration Offices set up in each country to accept submissions from the public on labour law matters have no subpoena power, can carry out no investigations in other countries in response to complaints, and can make their decisions based only on 'publicly available information'. While it is still too early to make a final judgement as to their effectiveness, their rulings to date have not inspired confidence in their ability genuinely to protect labour rights.[69]

The EU Social Chapter and Generalised System of Preferences (GSP)

The most advanced regional efforts at linking trade and labour standards have taken place within the European Union, which has progressively introduced legal requirements to enforce basic standards. The first European initiative came in 1950 with the Council of Europe's Social Charter, which drew heavily on existing ILO Conventions in setting out 19 rights and principles. In order to ratify the Charter, countries were obliged to bind themselves to comply with at least five of the seven core rights. But the Council of Europe's Charter was only declaratory and contained no implementing provisions. It was not until the late 1970s that some of these rights, such as equal pay, were tested and confirmed by the European Court of Justice.

As economic integration in Europe has intensified, so too has the pressure for the addition of a social dimension to market integration. In drafting proposals for the Social Chapter of the Maastricht Treaty, both the Economic and Social Committee and the European Commission drew heavily on ILO Conventions. The Commission paper of September 1988, for example, referred to no fewer than 60 ILO Conventions. The 13 basic rights incorporated into the Chapter, which was adopted by 11 member states in December 1989 (the UK having negotiated an opt-out clause), were all based either on ILO Conventions or the Council of Europe Charter. The internal EU debate therefore was essentially about implementing existing rights by means of European legislation.[70]

Outside Europe, of course, European law does not apply, and the EU has therefore considered the application of a social clause in various trade agreements with non-European countries. This was proposed by the EC in the first Lomé Convention with ACP countries during the 1970s, but the Lomé countries opposed it on the grounds that a social clause would infringe their national sovereignty.

Only recently has the EU introduced a bilateral social clause, in the form of its 1995 revised GSP scheme, which – under a waiver agreement from the WTO's Most Favoured Nation (MFN) principle – is based on preferential access rather than sanctions. The scheme offers additional preferences for countries which meet the requirements of ILO Conventions 87 and 98, relating to freedom of association and the right to organise, and Convention 138 relating to minimum-age employment. Controversy on the issue (and the opposition of the UK) has now led the Council of Ministers to delay implementation of these arrangements until 1998, and to call on the Commission to carry out, in 1997, a review of studies undertaken on the 'relationship between trade and labour rights' by the WTO, ILO, OECD, and other international fora.

Not until the findings of that review have been assessed will the degree of additional preference, and details of its application methods, be decided. (A similar procedure is envisaged for establishing the details of the preferential environmental clause, which is based on tropical timber standards alone.) A new 'withdrawal clause', specifying circumstances under which a developing country may be denied GSP treatment, has already come into effect, and criteria include the use of any form of forced labour or prison labour.

Much of the social incentive scheme, then, remains to be defined. In particular, it is not yet clear who will monitor the observation of the regulations. In the labour field, it would seem appropriate that the ILO take a lead role in assessing compliance with the standards and, with financial help from the EU, in monitoring the certification.

First indications are, however, that objective assessments of this scheme are being overshadowed by legitimate concerns over other aspects of the new GSP, including its limited product coverage, insufficient tariff cuts in areas of most relevance to poorer countries, and graduation measures.

Perhaps the most serious criticism which can be levelled at any positive or negative conditionality within any GSP scheme is that it is inevitably one-sided. The 'donors' are exclusively developed countries, and the 'beneficiaries' developing countries, thus reinforcing the suggestion that low environmental and labour standards are a problem for developing countries alone. This, clearly, is far from the case.

The US GSP

The social component of the US GSP scheme has been in place since 1985. Unlike the European proposals, it takes the form of a negative conditionality, setting out standards which all beneficiary countries must meet to be eligible for GSP treatment. Where the European model has a sliding tariff rate, with countries being rewarded for positive labour practices with an *additional* percentage of lower tariffs (the carrot rather than the stick), the US system operates a blanket tariff waiver which is withdrawn if countries do not meet certain standards (the withheld carrot).

These standards do not refer specifically to ILO Conventions (many of which the US has yet to ratify), but require countries to be 'taking steps to afford workers internationally-recognised workers' rights', including freedom of association, the right to collective bargaining, a prohibition against forced labour, a minimum age for work, and acceptable conditions of work related to wages, hours, health, and safety. Significantly, labour rights violations in any sector can lead to a challenge, with standards applying both to domestic production and to production linked to trade.

Petitions, which have mostly come from trade unions, are made to the US Administration claiming non-compliance with the provisions of the US legislation. The Administration then forms a Subcommittee made up of representatives from different departments, which reviews reports from within the US administration and from outside bodies, including the ILO. The Subcommittee can then either recommend a suspension of GSP preferences for the country concerned, dismiss the petition as unfounded, or call for an extended review procedure.

From 1985 to 1995 over 34 countries were named in petitions citing labour rights abuses under the US GSP law.[71] In most cases the petition was dismissed. In those cases when the petition was accepted, the normal course has been to give the country concerned time to change its behaviour. Out of 101 workers' rights petitions filed, only in 12 cases were preferences withdrawn or suspended.[72] This seems to indicate, as has been observed, that peer pressure is an effective form of enforcement, since extended reviews increase transparency and thus the pressure on a government which is denying basic labour rights. However, peer pressure with the threat of loss of preferences as an ultimate sanction is very different from peer pressure without it, as the ILO experience demonstrates.[73]

Indeed, trade unionists in countries under GSP review have claimed that their governments have responded to the criticisms in the GSP petition more seriously than they had ever reacted to a negative judgement by the ILO's Committee on Freedom of Association or Committee of Experts. In the Dominican Republic, for example, the threat of loss of GSP access to the US sugar market was enough to make the government crack down on the practice of enslaving Haitian workers in the country's sugar plantations, and reform its labour laws accordingly. As a result, the country never lost its GSP status. Workers in the plantations acquired the legal right to organise trade unions and to negotiate collective agreements. Today, however, new problems are being faced by these workers: the plantation owners are refusing to negotiate with the unions. Nevertheless, without the pressure of the GSP process, it is unlikely that the unions would even exist.[74]

There is plenty of evidence to suggest that arbitrary decisions also take place over GSP eligibility. For example, in 1993 the US Trade Representative refused to review Mexico and Colombia, two of the most serious abusers of workers' rights. (Mexico was at that time in negotiation for a Labour Side Agreement to NAFTA, and Colombia's President was the US candidate to head the Organisation of American States.) Similarly, in the case of countries, such as China, which are major sites for US investment or important markets for US exports, the US Trade Representative's office has been reluctant to act.

While conditionality in GSP systems can clearly play a role in helping to raise social standards, the one-sided nature and vulnerability to abuse of such systems makes conditionality within them both less effective and less equitable than a multilateral and transparent social clause binding all members of the international community.

The way forward

Bearing in mind the very legitimate concerns of developing countries, unions, and NGOs that the WTO is both untransparent and undemocratic, with no competence in labour issues and no representation from employers and workers, there are some very clear criteria which should apply to the selection and adoption of an appropriate mechanism within it. Oxfam would support the inclusion of a social clause only if the ILO is given the lead role in monitoring compliance and judging infringements. Such a clause should initially be restricted to Conventions 87 and 98 alone. The monitoring and enforcement procedure should be transparent and democratic, with recourse to sanctions only as a last resort.

Oxfam is therefore recommending that the first Ministerial Meeting of the WTO in Singapore in December 1996 takes the decision to set up a joint working party with the ILO, to make proposals on how the mechanisms for a jointly administered ILO/WTO social clause, initially focusing exclusively on ILO Conventions 87 and 98, would work in more detail, to report within a maximum of one year. Provision should be made for observer status to be accorded to a broad range of experts, including NGOs and citizens' groups from North and South, who should also be able to make written and oral input to committee proceedings. This provision should also be extended to organisations of 'informal' sector workers, such as homeworkers, who are neither formally recognised in their own right, nor adequately represented by trade unions.

When agreement has been reached on implementation of a social clause based on Conventions 87 and 98, the working party should extend its remit to consider the feasibility of including the other key human rights conventions (on discrimination, equal remuneration, and forced labour). Its terms of reference should include the establishment of effective mechanisms for the provision of financial and technical assistance for developing countries, and a petition mechanism to allow workers' groups from North and South to present complaints.

Genuine fears that the social clause represents no more than a disguised protectionist mechanism will need to be answered convincingly. In the framing of institutional mechanisms, therefore, it should be made clear that initial efforts would be concentrated on the resolution of disputes by mutual agreement. Any sanction would only be associated with countries that made no attempt, over a long period, to comply. Serious consideration should be given to the proposal that there should be a moratorium on any enforcement of standards through trade measures for a given period.[75] Such a moratorium would require developing countries to talk about standards rather than sanctions, and would give voluntary commitments a chance to work.

The Singapore meeting should also agree that the Trade Policy Reviews which the WTO prepares periodically on (and in collaboration with) individual Contracting Parties, should in future have a section on respect, or non-respect, for a voluntary code of fair labour practices drawn up in collaboration with, and monitored by, the ILO, based on the core human rights conventions 87, 98, 100, 111, 29, and 105.

CHAPTER THREE:
RECONCILING TRADE AND SUSTAINABLE DEVELOPMENT

Profits and pollution havens

Twelve years ago we came to live here. We thought we'd be in glory because it was an ecological reserve – lots of vegetation, animals, birds. Two years later the maquiladoras *started to arrive. Now many of us have skin problems – rashes, hair falling out, we get eye pains, fevers. My kids' legs are really bad – all the kids have nervous problems and on the way to school the dust and streams are all polluted.*

Maurilio Sanchez Pachuca, President of local Residents' Committee near Tijuana, Mexico[76]

In the last chapter we explored how international trade and foreign investment are integrating national economies and labour markets into an increasingly globalised system, and examined some of its negative effects on labour standards. There is a related danger, to which we will now turn: that the creation of 'pollution havens' will exercise downward pressure on environmental standards worldwide, as the fear of losing foreign investment or competitive advantage forces governments to lower environmental standards, or to resist raising them, or simply to refuse to enforce them. From Oxfam's perspective, however, unacceptably low environmental standards are not a source of legitimate comparative advantage, but a form of exploitation which can have devastating effects, as experience in the Mexican *maquiladora* region demonstrates.

The Mexican border region is the site of more than 2,000 manufacturing plants which operate by importing components free of duty, for assembly and re-export to the US. Blue-chip companies such as General Electric, General Motors, and Du Pont have all transferred plants to the *maquiladora* zone, attracted by a combination of lax enforcement of environmental laws and low labour costs. In the late 1980s, for example, the introduction of

67

more stringent air pollution controls in California prompted a large-scale exodus of furniture manufacturers to this region. More than a quarter of US firms with plants in Mexicali cited more stringent US environmental provisions as reasons for the relocation.[77]

The environmental costs of the *maquiladora* zone have been unacceptably high. According to Mexico's Secretariat of Urban Planning and Ecology, more than half of the *maquiladora* plants produce hazardous waste. This waste is supposed to be transferred to the United States, but compliance is the exception rather than the rule. An official of the Mexican Environment Ministry estimated in 1991 that only 35 per cent of the US-owned factories along the border comply with Mexican toxic-waste laws. The effect on public health has been appalling. In one investigation, the US National Toxics Campaign found heavy metals and other toxic discharges associated with birth defects and brain damage being emptied into open ditches running through settlements near the factories. The incidence of anencephalic (brainless) baby births in towns like Matamoros is 30 times the Mexican average. The American Medical Association has branded the *maquiladora* region 'a virtual cesspool and breeding ground for infectious diseases', with hepatitis and tuberculosis rife on both sides of the border.[78]

Workers trying to improve conditions have met head-on the harsh realities of unregulated foreign investment:

A group of us wanted to improve our working conditions, safety, and wages at Clarostat [a US company with a plant in Juarez, Mexico]. *We worked with dangerous chemicals, including phenol and epoxy resin, but no masks were provided. The chemicals irritated our skin. Six of us began to organise a union. We had meetings every two weeks. After a few months, another worker informed on me, and then I was fired. Four other workers were fired one week later. The personnel manager told me I was fired because I was trying to organise a union.*[79]

While the *maquiladoras* have received more incriminating publicity than other sites, they are, contrary to the claims of advocates of trade deregulation, far from unique. Environmentalists in

South-East Asia have criticised Japanese industries for allegedly locating extremely harmful processes abroad because they are environmentally unacceptable at home; while plenty of evidence points to the trend of pollution-intensive European chemical industries relocating to Asia in general, and China in particular. When the German chemical giant, Bayer, announced plans to transfer bulk capacity to Shanghai, the corporation's chief executive explained the move in terms of the disincentives to staying in Europe: 'The main disadvantage we have to face are higher labour costs and expensive social security systems, coupled with widespread regulation of environmental affairs by the state.'[80] The clear inference for governments in Europe, and even in other parts of South-East Asia, is that the price for retaining investment and employment is a progressive lowering of standards towards Chinese levels. Even the threat of potential relocation is enough to exercise a 'chilling' factor on standards.[81]

Moreover, there is every indication that the problem is likely to grow in the future, as the financial costs imposed by more stringent environmental regulation rise. The US Environmental Protection Agency estimates that US pollution control costs have gone from 0.9 per cent of GNP in 1972 to 2.1 per cent in 1990, and will rise to 2.8 per cent by 2000. In a US survey in 1991, senior executives of major corporations worldwide estimated that environmental costs averaged 2.4 per cent of total sales. But they expected it to rise to 4.3 per cent of sales by 2000.[82]

It is also significant that even when pollution control costs were lower, US inter-state competitiveness played an important role in the history of environmental protection: the establishment of national environmental law in the US was aimed at eliminating an environmental 'race to the bottom' among states eager for new investment and willing to compromise their pollution requirements for the sake of investment and jobs.[83]

The environmental degradation associated with trade liberalisation, which has accelerated under the North American Free Trade Agreement (NAFTA), offers a salutary warning of what might be anticipated under WTO-inspired trade and investment liberalisation. During the debate over the setting up of the NAFTA, Mexico promised to improve its enforcement mechanisms, and agreed to the explicit stipulation within the NAFTA Agreement that it is 'inappropriate' to relax environmental standards or enforcement in order to encourage investment. Unfortunately, this provision has little legal influence, and environmental groups are therefore lobbying to strengthen it. What is needed is the introduction of a legally binding provision to the same effect within the WTO framework, and a commitment to work towards internationally agreed minimum standards for some of the most polluting or environmentally damaging products and processes.

In the pages below, we will make the case that international trade rules should be reformed so that they can support, rather than undermine, efforts towards sustainable development.

International trade, economic growth, and the environment

In theory, the pursuit of international trade liberalisation and of environmental protection are quite compatible, since the efficient allocation of resources is integral to them both. According to the theory of comparative advantage, countries will specialise in the production of goods and services in which they are most efficient; this should mean that they are able to maximise their output from a given level of resource input, and therefore move towards conserving resources.

In addition, trade liberalisation can have significant positive effects on the environment, particularly in correcting the failure of trade policy interventions such as subsidies which encourage environmentally damaging activities, like those of the European Union's Common Agricultural Policy; and in facilitating international access to environmentally-friendly technology. Moreover, according to the advocates of free trade, the increased economic growth resulting from trade generates the funds needed to invest in environmental protection. Thus, according to Jagdish Bhagwati, the fear that the economic growth generated by free trade will harm the environment is misplaced. On the contrary: 'Growth enables governments to tax and raise resources for a variety of objectives, including the abatement of pollution and general protection of the environment.'[84]

The truth, of course, is considerably more complex: under certain conditions, a certain amount of certain kinds of international trade is beneficial; under others, it is undoubtedly harmful. The theory of comparative advantage is based on a number of assumptions, many of which are highly questionable. It assumes, for example, that prices reflect the true cost of production. Since this is rarely the case in practice (the prices of most commodities do not account for the environmental degradation caused by their production or extraction processes, for instance), economic inefficiencies will be generated, and countries' *real* comparative advantages will be mistaken. Under these conditions, trade can act to magnify unsustainable patterns of economic activity, and intensify problems of pollution and resource depletion.

Moreover, comparative advantages are not always equally dynamic: they are determined at a single point in time, but the long-term benefits of specialisation depend on the wider effects of stimulating the economy. The unequal benefits of specialising in, say, electronics and coffee, become frozen, with the coffee producers unable to diversify into higher value-added products, while the electronics producers can develop technological innovation and acquire new labour skills. Specialisation patterns are often divided along North-South lines, with many of the poorest developing countries unable to break out of a dependence on commodities (tariff escalation is discussed on p.13).

The theory of comparative advantage also assumes that the factors of production are not internationally mobile, so that each country's capital and labour stays exclusively within its own borders. Today, the increasing mobility of capital means that factors of production travel according to the logic of absolute advantage, or simple price competitiveness, leading to pressure on those countries without such advantage to reduce labour and environmental standards and investment regulations, in a bid to increase their own competitiveness.[85]

Furthermore, while the finance generated by increasing trade *could* be spent on environmental protection, it would require an extraordinary leap of faith to assume that it necessarily would be. Higher national income does not automatically lead to reduced environmental degradation;[86] and when the cost of the environmental degradation caused in the very process of pursuing further trade and economic growth exceeds the revenue generated by it, then it is clear that trade cannot be said to be beneficial for the environment.

This situation is increasingly likely to occur, particularly in respect of environmental costs of energy use, which are seldom taken into account in assessments of the true costs of production. Those energy costs associated with the transport sector are perhaps the most significant, since the link between increased trade and increased transport is largely undisputed.[87] While energy use might become more efficient, the effect of that is likely to be outweighed by the greater overall volume of journeys. As the EC Task Force on the Single Market itself concluded: 'The favourable environmental effects of efficiency in the use of resources are likely to be outweighed by the growth in demand, with consequent increases in environmental pressures.'[88]

An analytical framework developed by the OECD to examine the potential environmental effects of trade, and trade liberalisation, usefully distinguishes between effects in terms of scale, products, structure, and regulation.[89] An examination of scale effects confirms that while it is in theory easier to raise levels of environmental protection in a growing economy, the empirical evidence, as demonstrated by a study of regional trade liberalisation and the transport sector, reveals that levels of freight transport, primarily on roads, will increase at a rate faster than economic growth in the countries concerned.

Most significant, however, is the OECD's recognition that the regulations associated with trade liberalisation can themselves have a damaging effect on the environment. Its conclusion – that positive regulatory effects can be assured from trade liberalisation 'if care is taken not to undermine the ability of governments to pursue appropriate and effective environmental policies' – encapsulates the heart of the problem. For it is the argument of this chapter that current WTO rules provide an inadequate framework for sustainable development precisely because they *do* undermine governments' ability to legislate in favour of environmental sustainability.

The OECD's own analysis identifies the fact that environmental values are not fully reflected in the prices of traded goods as one of the major negative effects of trade liberalisation. Yet current trade rules discourage governments from pursuing a strategy of internalising costs precisely because they prohibit governments from protecting their domestic industry from cheaper competition from countries who have not internalised costs to the same extent.

The traditional defence of free trade is that the cause of environmental degradation is not trade liberalisation, but a failure to price a country's environmental resources correctly, with trade simply acting as a 'magnifier' of that failure. But this argument fails to recognise that attempts by countries to rectify faulty pricing policies are frequently blocked *by the regulatory system itself*. In the real world, cost internalisation rarely occurs: externalities prevail, and to develop a trade theory and policy on the basis that they do not exist or are internalised is therefore somewhat perverse.[90]

The WTO: an inadequate framework for sustainable development

One of the most fundamental problems in sustainable trade management is that the WTO is premised on rules which reflect a very narrowly defined market framework. For example, WTO Articles expressly prohibit the use of subsidies on the grounds that subsidies distort markets. This leads to the prohibition of 'dumping', whereby it is forbidden to sell a product on the international market at less than its normal domestic price. However, environmental degradation itself increasingly imposes real costs which are not reflected in market prices, and this has a similar distorting effect on trade as dumping or subsidisation.

For example, thousands of tons of fungicides, herbicides, and insecticides are washed from intensively farmed arable fields into groundwater supplies, rivers, and coastal waters each year. For the UK alone, it has been estimated that it would cost £450 million to reduce levels of pesticide residues in drinking water to EU standards. However, this cost is not incorporated into the price of crops grown under these conditions. Neither are the wider 'non-market' costs resulting from the loss of wildlife habitats, such as meadows, woods, and hedgerows.

The WTO framework as currently constituted fails to recognise this. Although Article XX (b) and (g) appear to offer significant scope for the protection of the environment and the health of living things by permitting measures 'necessary to protect human, animal or plant life or health', and 'relating to the conservation of exhaustible natural resources', that scope has in fact been severely limited by various restrictive interpretations. Measures relating to process and production methods in other countries, or to health and the environment outside a country's own territory and jurisdiction, are not permitted. Furthermore, the term 'necessary' in Article XX (b) has been narrowly defined as 'least GATT-inconsistent'; and it is not clear whether the 'exhaustible resources' of Article XX (g) can be construed to include the atmosphere and oceans, so they may not be covered under this article, even if territoriality considerations allowed.[91]

Some of these limitations were vividly demonstrated in the notorious 'tuna/dolphin' panel decision which ruled that the US ban on Mexican-caught tuna was illegal under GATT rules, not only because it was discriminatory (which, in the way that it was implemented, it probably was), but also on the more far-reaching grounds that it related to process and production methods, not products, and because the US was seeking to apply its laws outside its own jurisdiction.[92] The assumption appears to be that since the GATT treaty was negotiated between national governments, its mandate covers only national jurisdictions. Yet the lessons of sustainable development show that environmental problems are increasingly transnational and cannot be addressed by a framework based on nation states alone.

The challenge, then, is how to incorporate concerns of sustainable development into the WTO? The conventional economic school of thought would simply argue that the Uruguay Round Agreement is a treaty whose strength lies in expanding world trade, and therefore any attempt to address non-trade issues will inevitably lead to market distortion and the threat of protectionist abuse.

This is a very curious argument, however, in view of the recognition by many of those same economists that economic growth is itself generating significant costs; and indeed a very inconsistent one, in view of the urgent calls from the World Bank and others for countries to adopt price-related measures nationally to reduce environmental costs. A recent World Bank report, *East Asia's Environment: Principles and Priorities for Action* notes that:

Environmental problems require attention because markets alone cannot be relied on to reduce excessive damage to the environment...The costs to society that come from pollution and the degradation of natural resources are not automatically taken into account in the decision of businesses, governments and individuals.

The report concludes that governments should ensure that environmental costs are incorporated into both private and public policy decisions. But if there is a logic to incorporating environmental costs into economic decision-making nationally, a similar logic must apply internationally, or else economic relations at the international level would be subject to the same market distortions as the World Bank is concerned to address at the national level.

When one country internalises costs to a greater degree than another, it is likely to suffer competitive disadvantage, since its cost of production will probably rise. One way to counter this effect would be to set a floor of certain internationally agreed minimum environmental standards to which all countries must adhere. Many developing countries, however, fear that if the WTO were to be used to establish minimum standards, it could encourage protectionist abuse. They point out, with considerable justification, that poverty is the real cause of low standards; and they claim that access to Northern markets is vital to raising these standards. Yet the pursuit of trade expansion without regard to ecological constraints is likely to intensify poverty and prove disastrous to present and future generations alike.

It is clear that complete harmonisation of environmental standards is neither practical nor desirable, but moving towards some minimum parity level for some of the most environmentally-damaging production processes would be a step towards placing international trade on more sustainable foundations. The setting of environmental standards should not be undertaken by the WTO itself, since it has neither mandate nor competence in this area, but by another mechanism or body with the appropriate expertise, which would be transparent, democratic, and accountable; possibly a body established under the auspices of the CSD or a new Intergovernmental Panel on Trade and Sustainable Development (see pp. 92-3).

Clearly, many developing countries would be unable to afford the clean technologies needed to meet higher environmental standards. The Brundtland Commission estimated that in the early

1980s developing countries exporting to the OECD countries would have incurred costs in excess of $5 billion if they had been required to meet US standards. The sum today would be considerably larger. That means that financial resource transfers, including debt relief, will need to be linked to the adoption of technologies that would enable developing countries to introduce higher standards. Similarly, where tariffs are deployed to protect industries meeting higher environmental standards, the revenue generated must be repatriated to developing countries in the form of an environment fund, administered by a multilateral body, for investment in clean technologies. It should be a priority for the international community in general, and the WTO's Committee on Trade and Environment in particular, to investigate a range of mechanisms to achieve this, drawing on advice and experience from all appropriate intergovernmental bodies, NGOs, and citizens' groups in both the South and the North alike.[93]

Multilateral environmental agreements

Setting minimum standards through international agreement is clearly preferable to unilateral action, and the negotiation of multilateral environmental agreements (MEAs) should therefore be encouraged. Prominent examples of MEAs which employ trade restrictions to enforce compliance include the Convention on International Trade in Endangered Species (CITES), the Basel Convention on the Control of the Transboundary Movement of Hazardous Wastes and Their Disposal, and the Montreal Protocol on Substances that Deplete the Ozone Layer. Those MEAs which lack trade provisions, such as those related to sustainable fisheries management, have been considerably less successful.

However, trade measures within these agreements raise the prospect of inconsistency with WTO rules, notably the Article XI prohibition on quantitative restrictions on international trade, or the provisions of Articles I and III concerning national treatment and non-discrimination. This potential inconsistency is likely to inhibit implementation of existing MEAs, and the negotiation of future ones. The WTO Agreement should therefore be amended to permit trade measures as set out in broadly based international environment agreements. This could follow the model of the NAFTA which specifically allows that, in most cases where conflict arises between its own provision and those of MEAs, the latter shall take precedence.

Although multilateral action through MEAs is clearly more desirable (and usually more effective) than unilateral trade measures, MEAs are often difficult and time-consuming to negotiate and implement. The GATT tuna/dolphin panel seemed unaware, for example, that the US had been trying to negotiate an international agreement on the protection of dolphins from damaging fishing practices since 1972. It is therefore necessary to consider in what circumstances unilateral trade measures can legitimately be employed in the pursuit of sustainable development. These are explored below, together with the reforms of WTO trade rules that would be required to facilitate them.

Ways forward

There are various ways in which the problem of loss of competitiveness could be addressed in the absence of internationally agreed minimum standards. Border tax adjustment, for example, involves adjusting the price of imports and exports at the border to ensure that products and processes are subject to the same degree of environmental taxation regardless of origin. WTO rules allow adjustment for domestic taxes levied on products, but appear not to allow it for those imposed on the basis of production and processing methods. The obstacle which this ambiguity puts in the way of sustainable development has been vividly demonstrated by the resistance which accompanied proposals by the European Commission to establish a carbon/energy tax. The European governments decided to postpone any further consideration of them until the implications for the competitiveness of European industry could be addressed. Border tax adjustment would be one way of enabling energy costs to rise without penalising domestic industry.

The ambiguity surrounding WTO rules on this issue stems primarily from the terms of the Subsidies and Countervailing

Measures Agreement concluded in the Uruguay Round. Footnote 61 to Annex II of this Agreement appears to extend the scope of WTO rules to allow for the adjustment of indirect taxes on energy inputs.[94]

There is dissent within the international community, however, on how this note should be interpreted. The current agenda of the WTO's Committee on Trade and Environment (CTE) includes a discussion of 'charges and taxes for environmental purposes' and therefore provides a crucial opportunity to address this issue, and to make genuine progress towards sustainable development. The concerns of developing countries should be central to the debate. Any obligations on poorer countries to meet industrial country environmental standards would need to be linked to the provision of financial support, and the revenue generated by tax adjustment remitted back to developing countries, to be invested in cleaner technologies.

An alternative mechanism has been proposed, which avoids the difficulties in calculating full border tax adjustment and full cost-internalisation, but at the same time removes the influence of competitiveness concerns from environmental policy-making. Paul Ekins suggests that companies that can show genuine disadvantage from environmental policies should be able to protect themselves from the effects for a limited period while they adjust to the new reality.[95] He proposes that WTO rules should be changed to enable individual countries to levy countervailing duties on imported products (or give rebates to exported products) where the domestic industry concerned can demonstrate that its products suffer a competitive disadvantage due to domestic environmental legislation.

Strict conditions are proposed: the environmental problem must be global or transboundary; the duties are time-limited (say, three years); levels must be based on an independent assessment of the real costs to the industry; a minimum threshold of competitive disadvantage would have to shown (for example, 5 per cent on the price of a product); and a notice period for the measures would be required, during which they would be open to challenge. In addition, revenue derived from the countervailing duties would be placed in a fund to help developing countries to improve the environmental performance of their economies.

Process and production methods (PPMs)

Under current WTO rules, countries are permitted to ban the import of products which will harm their own environments, as long as the standards applied are non-discriminatory between countries, and between domestic and foreign production. However, as the tuna/dolphin case revealed, a country cannot discriminate against imports on the basis of the way in which they are produced. In the absence of a multilateral environmental agreement, a country is not permitted to take any unilateral trade measure to protect its environment from foreign production, or to protect the environment outside its own jurisdiction, whether a global commons or the territory of another country, from damage caused by a PPM. This makes little sense, however, since from an environmental point of view, there is no meaningful distinction to be drawn between the environmental harm which is generated by a product, or the harm generated by its process and production methods: it is clear that regulations should be equally applicable to both sources of environmental damage.

Not only does this artificial distinction between products and PPMs undermine attempts to move towards sustainable development, it is also highly inconsistent with other WTO Articles. Both the Agreement on Subsidies and Countervailing Measures and the Agreement on Trade-Related Aspects of Intellectual Property Rights regulate some aspects of how goods are produced, allowing importing countries to discriminate against products if they are produced using excessive subsidy or misappropriated intellectual property.[96] Furthermore, Article XX (e) allows countries to discriminate against products made by prison labour.

There is no reason why a consistent, rules-based approach to PPMs could not be agreed, which would set out objective criteria under which trade measures directed against PPMs could be taken.[97] At a minimum, it should be possible to agree conditions under which unilateral action is permissible when the environmental damage caused by the PPM has a physical impact on the country concerned, either on its own territory or through its interest in the global commons. Such conditions could include:

- Evidence of significant physical environmental damage.[98]
- Evidence that the country concerned has attempted to resolve the issue through negotiations with potentially affected trading partners.
- Due notice (e.g. 12 months) of intention to introduce trade measures in support of environmental policies to be given, during which international agreement should be sought which would make the measures unnecessary.
- Measures must be non-discriminatory between foreign and domestic producers or products, and proportionate to the problem addressed.

It may also be possible to go further, and agree certain conditions under which governments could be permitted to take unilateral action even if the locus of damage appears to be wholly in another country: for example, countering competitive effects caused by PPMs which do not internalise costs, on a temporary basis, as suggested above. This is clearly a very sensitive issue, raising legitimate fears about possible protectionist abuse, not least because of the GATT's and now WTO's justified reputation for secrecy, untransparency, and lack of democracy. It would therefore be neither feasible nor appropriate to pursue it until the WTO's methods of operation were dramatically reformed. However, just as international law already recognises the principle of adherence to certain international standards of behaviour in the area of human rights legislation, for example, there is no legal reason why this should not also extend to certain ways of treating the environment.

An alternative proposal, which acknowledges that many developing countries (and others) lack confidence in the WTO, is to establish an Intergovernmental Panel on Trade and Sustainable

Development (IPTSD) (see p.92-93). Such a forum would be more open and democratic than the WTO, and have an overriding commitment to sustainable development, rather than pursuing trade expansion alone.

The panel would focus on multi-disciplinary analysis and policy formulation, which would build on and unite the working relationships which are developing between the relevant agencies of the UN, other international bodies, governments, academic institutions, and NGOs. While it would not have decision-making powers over the WTO, it would have a moral authority, a strong capacity for public persuasion and peer pressure, and a recognised expertise in its field.[99] One of its tasks could be to undertake country studies on production processes, with a view to assessing, and making public, any instances of continued gross externalisation of environmental costs. The resulting publicity might in itself be sufficient to persuade the government or industry in question to raise their standards; if not, the Panel could research, and make recommendations on, the most appropriate trade and other policy measures (such as debt relief) to be taken.

Dispute settlement mechanisms

The sensitivity surrounding the issue of trade measures in support of sustainable development makes it crucial that the WTO has a procedure for settling disputes which is transparent and accountable, and which enjoys the confidence of all Contracting Parties. It should also integrate sustainable development objectives into both the principles and procedures for resolving disputes between members. The *Understanding on Rules and Procedures Governing the Settlement of Disputes* (DSU), incorporated into the Final Act of the Uruguay Round, establishes an integrated disputes settlement mechanism with much greater scope and power than the former GATT mechanisms.

The DSU represents a significant advance in many ways, including the introduction of expert review groups (which could include experts on environmental issues and sustainable development), an increased role for arbitration, and an appeals process. However, it still fails to offer provision for adequate public information. Most importantly, the DSU must ensure that all parties, whatever their economic influence on world trade, are bound by the rule of law. Without this, there is a serious risk that the developed countries will continue to use (or will be perceived to be continuing to use) the system to their own ends, selling an increasing volume of goods and services in emerging developing country markets, while keeping their own markets closed to developing country goods through a variety of protectionist barriers.[100]

Sustainable natural resource management

Around 25 per cent of world trade involves the import and export of primary products, such as timber, fish, minerals, tea, and coffee. Many of the world's poorest countries are heavily dependent upon such exports for their foreign exchange earnings. The environmental costs of such exports are not accounted for in the price of the commodity, nor do they figure in national accounting systems.

The huge increase in shellfish exports from developing countries is a case in point. During the 1980s, production of shrimps in Asia underwent a phenomenal growth, jumping from 57,000 to over 441,000 tonnes per annum. The foreign exchange gains have been substantial. By 1990, shellfish was the largest non-oil commodity export from developing countries and for some of the poorest countries, such as Vietnam and Bangladesh, shellfish exports are now one of their largest sources of foreign exchange. However, shrimp and shellfish farming are also having disastrous environmental consequences.

In many areas of Bangladesh, the expansion of shrimp farming for export has been achieved by the transformation of vast tracts of agricultural land into shrimp ponds. The effect on local communities has been dramatic. In some cases, peasant farmers have found their rice crops ruined and their water supply contaminated by salt water leaking into their fields from neighbouring shrimp farms. Even the more amicable land-share arrangements, whereby land is leased to a shrimp farmer for part of the year for the shrimp production cycle, before being returned to the owner for the rest of the year, have had serious environmental impacts. Rice farmers who lease their land claim that the increase in salinity required for shrimp cultivation has reduced rice yields by two-thirds. They believe it will take many years to restore the land's fertility. Sometimes land belonging to others is deliberately flooded. This increases soil salinity, and reduces fertility, undermining the livelihoods of small producers. Owners are then left with little choice but to rent their land out at rock-bottom prices. In the words of one Bangladeshi farmer:

Before, we used to have cows in our sheds and rice in our houses. We used to be able to catch sweetwater fish in our ponds. But now we have none of these things.[101]

Forcible displacement of smallholder producers has often involved considerable violence. In addition, the demands of the shrimp industry for fresh water have severely depressed the water table in many areas, creating water shortages and adding to the problems of salinity.

In the Philippines, mangrove swamps have been cleared at an average rate of 3,000 hectares a year to make way for large commercial prawn farms, most of them owned by companies producing for export to Japan. Mangrove swamps now cover less than one-tenth of their original area. The destruction of the mangroves, which provided breeding grounds for fish, has resulted in a progressive lowering of fish catches each year for local fishing communities. If current trends continue, the Philippines' remaining mangrove swamps will be destroyed within a decade. Oxfam is supporting the efforts of local people in the Philippines to protect their common natural resources from commercial encroachment, combining practical action aimed at reversing the trend of declining fish catches with advocacy to press for the creation of an equitable and environmentally sustainable regulatory framework.

But action at the international level is also needed, to create an enabling framework within which national governments can pursue sustainable development policies. Current prices for natural products like shrimps do not reflect the environmental costs of production. This undervaluation leads directly to overuse and depletion of natural resources. The prices charged by Japanese companies to consumers for shrimps, for example, do not reflect the huge costs to local communities of lost fish stocks, and reduced soil fertility, nor the consequent loss of livelihoods. In theory, governments could intervene in markets to ensure that prices more accurately reflect the true costs, by imposing consumption taxes or import levies on unsustainably produced materials; or, in extreme cases, by prohibiting imports.

The international trade rules enshrined in the WTO, which do not allow for the imposition of consumption or import taxes on the grounds of unsustainable production, therefore act as a potential restraint on local and international action to protect natural resources, undermining the ability of governments to regulate in favour of sustainable development, and disempowering local communities in their struggle for a better environment.

Nor is it clear whether they permit export controls in the interest of sustainable resource management. While existing rules allow governments to restrict exports for environmental reasons, such restrictions are treated as exemptions to free trade which are only granted under stringent conditions. Recourse to GATT has been used to overturn existing conservation measures, forcing a reversal of Canada's fish-stock-management policies in the early 1980s, for example. Similarly, the Dutch government withdrew its initiative to promote an EU ban on unsustainably-logged timber, following warnings that it could be inconsistent with GATT obligations.

There are clearly serious conflicts between the rules of international trade and the demands of sustainable resource management. This is an area in which WTO rules should be reformed. In certain circumstances, export prohibition can play an important role in sustainable resource management. So can export taxes and import levies, as outlined above. Applied in an open and non-discriminatory manner, such market instruments could significantly enhance the prospects for more sustainable trade across a wide range of products.

Case study: Promotion of a sustainable banana trade

For some of the world's poorest and most vulnerable producers, the failure of the Uruguay Round to address environmental problems is being compounded by the damaging impact of its rules on existing trade arrangements. The experience of banana producers in the Caribbean provides an example of such effects.

Until 1992, the EU banana market reflected the old colonial ties of its member states. Britain, for example, imported two-thirds of its bananas from its former colonies in the Caribbean, including the Windward Islands. But this arrangement could only be maintained by protecting the British market from Latin American exporters, where bananas are produced at around half of the cost of those from the Caribbean, on giant, highly mechanised estates.

The introduction of the Single European Market (SEM) in 1992 made such protection inconsistent with EU law. After a lengthy debate, however, in July 1993 Europe introduced a new import policy which set an increased quota for Latin American bananas. Imports above that quota – set at 2 million tons – were to be subject to higher duties. The EU's policy of safeguarding preferential access for ACP bananas was justified by the overwhelming dependence of Caribbean exporters on the EU market. In the Windward Islands, bananas account for 15 per cent of national income and over half of export earnings. Around 57,000 people, a third of the labour force, are directly or indirectly involved in the banana industry. It was therefore vital to maintain a viable banana industry in a region where unemployment is in excess of 20 per cent and where there are few economic alternatives.

The subsequent GATT challenge over the new EU regime brought by five Latin American exporters resulted in a ruling that discrimination against the Latin American countries was a violation of the obligation on the EU to uphold the GATT principle of Most Favoured Nation (MFN) treatment. More recently, in September 1995, following a complaint from the giant US banana corporation, Chiquita Brands International, the US Trade Representative filed a complaint with the WTO, which is currently under consideration.

It is clear that serious issues lie at the heart of this dispute. There are legitimate discussions to be had over whether trade preferences are the most appropriate way of supporting the livelihoods of poor people, and whether preferential agreements based on former colonial ties unfairly exclude other, possibly even poorer, nations. However, whatever the problems associated with market regulation, it is highly questionable to suggest that these problems will be resolved, and social and environmental well-being improved, simply by a lurch towards market deregulation.

From Oxfam's own experience based on working with partner groups over many years, we know that if the complaint against the EU were upheld, it would have a devastating effect on the livelihoods of thousands of people in the Caribbean, who currently enjoy few other employment opportunities. The WTO should therefore recognise the right of nations to put peoples' welfare above corporate self-interest and free trade, and rule against the complaint.

That is not to say, however, that the current EU banana regime is not in need of reform. Current methods of banana cultivation carry high social and environmental costs. Like many crop farmers, banana producers have been struggling for higher yields per acre, partly to meet increased demand, but also in order to lower unit costs of production. Producers are also under pressure to produce more uniform fruit with fewer blemishes. All of this leads to higher inputs of fertilisers, nematicides, and above all, fungicides. The haphazard practice of aerial spraying has become the norm, while chemical-impregnated polythene sleeves (which are supposed to protect the fruit from a variety of diseases) litter the fields. Laws stipulating that the natural vegetation should be left intact along water-courses are ignored, and pesticide residues build up in soils, in fresh water, and on coral reefs along the coast.

In the Windward Islands, the drive to increase production has meant that steeper slopes are being cultivated, increasing the risk of soil erosion. In Latin America, increased areas devoted to plantations have led to a loss of both farmland and forest. These large acreages, all devoted to one variety of crop, represent an environmental problem in themselves, since they provide no variety of habitats for associated wildlife, while at the same time they create optimum conditions for pests. A typical response to this is to blanket large areas with pesticides, causing further problems.

In the light of the ongoing social and environmental problems associated with banana production in the South, the EU – as the world's largest single importer – has a particular responsibility to encourage improved sustainability in the banana sector. One method open to the EU is the application of minimum criteria for sustainable production in trade regimes such as the EU's Single European Market for bananas, with a positive trade incentive given to those producers who produce in a more sustainable way.

A European network of NGOs, supported by Oxfam, working with banana producers has made proposals for the reform of the European banana regime in order to create a quota for bananas which have been produced in a fair and environmentally sustainable way.[102] The proposals include a core package of minimum social and environmental standards, and a measurement for sustainability certification; but they are being blocked by European Commission claims that such reform would be contrary to current WTO rules which do not allow discrimination on the basis of the way in which products have been produced.

Such rules make it almost impossible to put the banana trade onto a more sustainable basis, and improve the environmental and social impact of production. Research should therefore be undertaken urgently to establish criteria under which world trade rules could permit discrimination on the basis of the way products have been produced, as proposed above. The EU should modify EU Regulation 404/93 in such a way as to allow preferential market access for fairly and sustainably produced bananas.

Institutional reform

This chapter has made the case that the WTO, as currently constituted, does not offer an effective framework for the regulation of international trade in the interests of sustainable development. Reforms are urgently needed to make it into a framework which protects the environment, and the basic rights of people, without jeopardising legitimate trade interests. Such a framework should not be developed by trade ministers in the WTO alone, but by a wider forum which is more democratic and transparent, and which is committed to sustainable development, rather than solely to trade expansion.

At its Second Session, in May 1994, the Commission on Sustainable Development (CSD), which was set up to monitor progress on environmental issues after the Rio Earth Summit, undertook to review annually 'developments in the area of trade, development, and environment, with a view to identifying possible gaps and to promote co-operation and co-ordination' (Chair's Report, 1994). It also recognised that 'there is considerable need for improvement' in the areas of transparency, openness, and the active involvement of the public and experts, in relation to work on trade and environment.

At its Third Session, in April 1995, the CSD reiterated the importance both of co-ordination and of transparency, and invited UNCTAD to:

...*review the growing volume of research on trade, environment and sustainable development linkages carried out by international organisations, as well as academic institutions and non-governmental organisations in developed and developing countries... with a view to identifying possible gaps, including through the use of independent trade and environment expert groups.*

This is an important step forward, which acknowledges that no one institution has the mandate or the expertise to perform the full range of analysis that will be needed on the interface between trade, environment, and sustainable development. It still falls short of a forum in which cross-sectoral policies can be analysed and discussed by a range of experts from both North and South.

There has been some welcome progress in the level of co-operation between institutions working on different aspects of the trade, environment, and sustainable development agenda. The Trade and Environment Committee of the WTO has extended observer status to a wide range of international bodies including the CSD, UNCTAD, UNEP, and the World Bank (although little progress has yet been seen in relation to the involvement of NGOs), while UNEP and UNCTAD in particular have deepened their co-operation on related issues.

However, UNEP and UNCTAD are constrained by the parameters of their mandates, and the WTO suffers from a narrowly-defined free-market remit. While it is formally democratic, the WTO will nevertheless reflect the imbalances in trading power between the North and the South, with the world's poorest countries continuing to be confined to the margins of decision-making. There is still no interdisciplinary forum where representatives from governments, international bodies, academics, and NGOs from North and South can participate together in debate and analysis on the complex relationships between trade, environment, and development.

Oxfam and others therefore believe that there is an urgent need to establish an Intergovernmental Panel on Trade and Sustainable Development (IPTSD) to focus on multi-disciplinary analysis and policy formulation.[103] One of the chief benefits of such a panel would be the opportunity it would offer to analyse both trade and non-trade policy mechanisms relevant to sustainable development, in the same forum. Such non-trade mechanisms include investment flows, technology transfer, debt relief, and national and international development policies. Only within this broader perspective will it be possible to agree an effective international framework within which all countries would have the capacity and the opportunity to achieve sustainable development.

The IPTSD should have a broad, open-ended mandate to explore the trade, environment, and sustainable development interface. The Panel's first priorities should be to:

- initiate a full impact assessment of the Uruguay Round Agreement on the environment and sustainable development, and develop recommendations for change in the event of negative impacts being identified;
- explore, and make recommendations to the CSD and to the WTO Committee on Trade and Environment on potential cross-sectoral mechanisms to integrate trade, environment, and sustainable development objectives;
- develop policy instruments to achieve commodity prices which reflect the true environmental and social cost of their production;
- develop recommendations on meeting the needs of developing countries for technical and financial assistance in the design, utilisation, and response to trade measures and technical regulations;
- research, and make proposals on, the criteria under which unilateral trade measures may be taken, including development of the concept of 'green tariffication', whereby if tariffs are deployed to protect industries meeting higher environmental standards, the revenue generated could be repatriated to developing countries in the form of an environment fund, administered by a multilateral body, for investment in appropriate technologies.

CHAPTER FOUR: AGENDA FOR REFORM
The case for reform

During the post-war period, international trade flows have expanded by a factor of twelve, to over $4.0 trillion, and have played an important role in increasing global prosperity. Since the early 1980s, for example, international trade has grown by 50 per cent more than the growth of global GNP, so that imports and exports are increasingly prominent in the economic activity of most countries. The global stock of foreign investment has grown even faster, tripling in size since the 1980s.

While many have benefited from this expansion, a growing number of people in both North and South have become increasingly marginalised, and are paying heavily for the social and environmental costs which expanding world trade is bringing in its wake. This report has made the case that world trade rules are in urgent need of reform, in order to protect people's basic rights and to safeguard the environment. The most urgent of these reforms are summarised below.

There are a number of opportunities for pursuing this agenda for reform: one of the earliest and most critical will be the first Ministerial Meeting of the WTO which takes place in Singapore at the end of 1996, where further discussion of trade and labour links is likely, together with a review of the progress made by the WTO's Committee on Trade and Environment (CTE). The ongoing work of the CTE, discussions within the ILO, and the growing involvement of the CSD in the trade and sustainable development debate offer other important opportunities.

International regulation of trade and labour standards

- ◆ As an urgent priority, a joint ILO/WTO working party should be set up to make recommendations on implementation mechanisms for a multilateral social clause which would meet the criteria set out in chapter two above, to focus initially on

Conventions 87 and 98 (Freedom of Association and the Right to Organise and Collective Bargaining).

♦ The WTO should include, in its regular Trade Policy Reviews, a section on compliance with a set of fair labour practices, based on the core human rights conventions, drawn up in collaboration with, and monitored by, the ILO (see p. 48).

♦ The ILO's Freedom of Association procedure (whereby governments are subject to examination regardless of whether they have ratified the instrument in question) should be extended to cover the Conventions on discrimination and forced labour.

♦ Governments should support the proposed new ILO Convention on Homeworking (which would extend labour law protection to homeworkers) when it is discussed at the ILO's Annual Conference in June 1996, and ratify it as soon as possible thereafter.

International regulation of trade and sustainable development

♦ The Uruguay Round Agreements should be amended in such a way as to recognise the right of governments to use trade measures (provided that the measures are non-discriminatory, necessary, and proportional) in pursuit of sustainable development. In particular, the WTO treaty should be amended so as to permit trade measures as set out in Multilateral Environment Agreements (MEAs), or in the pursuit of internationally agreed environmental standards. Such standards should be reached in a transparent, participatory, and equitable way, by a body with appropriate environment and development expertise. Neither the WTO nor the International Organisation for Standardisation (ISO) meet these requirements, and are not therefore acceptable bodies for this purpose. A body set up under the auspices of the CSD, or an Intergovernmental Panel on Trade and Sustainable Development, might offer a more appropriate forum for this task. MEAs must contain provisions for financial and technical support to developing countries.

- The WTO treaty should also be amended to enable countries to impose import/export levies and consumption taxes in the interests of sustainable development, and to allow governments, under agreed circumstances, to implement trade restrictions where production and processing methods are having adverse environmental consequences, or where these measures are necessary to maintain higher domestic environmental standards. Trade rules should permit legitimate border tax adjustment to compensate for energy or pollution taxes imposed on domestic industries. Obligations on developing countries to comply with higher standards should be linked to the provision of technical and financial support, including debt relief, and be subject to longer transitional periods than for the industrialised countries.

- The terms of reference for the WTO's Committee on Trade and Environment (CTE) should be extended to encompass the broader concept of sustainable development, and widened to include collaboration with other appropriate intergovernmental agencies (including UNEP, UNCTAD, and the CSD), as well as with NGOs and citizens' groups from North and South.

- The CTE should recommend the withdrawal of escalating tariffs on primary commodities exported from developing countries, and support the investigation of ways of internalising environmental costs into the price of commodities by using non-discriminatory positive incentives such as ICREAs (International Commodity-Related Environmental Agreements), in collaboration with ongoing work in UNCTAD.[104]

- The CTE should agree a process (to involve consultation with all appropriate intergovernmental bodies, NGOs and citizens' groups) to establish a mechanism whereby revenue generated by tariffs which have been deployed in the interests of sustainable development can be pooled in an environment fund, administered by a multilateral body, for investment in clean technologies in developing countries.

- *Food security*: The WTO and regional trade association rules should be reformed to allow developing countries to protect their food systems up to the point of food self-sufficiency for social, ecological and economic reasons. The development of a food security clause for the WTO and regional trade groupings should be a priority for the FAO's 1996 World Food Summit agenda.

◆ More effective WTO rules to prohibit the dumping of agricultural surpluses should be introduced. Artificial distinctions between 'market intervention' measures and 'non-trade-distorting' subsidies have institutionalised in the WTO levels of subsidised overproduction and export dumping which would be unthinkable in other sectors of international trade. A clearer definition is needed of export subsidisation for agriculture, consistent with the wider anti-dumping provisions of the WTO: namely that products should not be marketed overseas at prices below their cost of production at home.

◆ *Intellectual Property Rights:* The CTE should affirm that in the event of a conflict between the WTO and the Biodiversity Convention, the Convention's provisions will prevail. It should also establish a review procedure for examining the implications of the TRIPS agreement for sustainable development, in consultation with the relevant UN bodies, NGOs, and local communities, as well as industry. At the same time, new mechanisms of development assistance need to be pursued to facilitate the transfer of technologies to developing countries, allied to measures which curb the restrictive practices of TNCs in relation to technology transfer.

◆ The United Nations Commission on Sustainable Development should continue and expand its active role in international discussions on trade, environment and development. A decision at the Commission's second session in May 1994 affirmed the need for the CSD to 'interact with the World Trade Organisation in future work' on trade and the environment. The CSD should provide guidance to the WTO (and particularly the CTE) on WTO reforms needed to implement the objectives set out in Agenda 21 for protection of the environment, sustainable development, public participation and transparency. Interaction between the CTE and the CSD would offer a useful means by which the WTO committee can incorporate the principles of the Rio Declaration and Agenda 21 into its work, as proposed by the Uruguay Round Ministerial Decision on Trade and Environment.

◆ Governments of industrialised countries should consider ways of reducing currently unsustainable levels of production and consumption, in consultation with exporting countries that might be affected by such changes.

Impact assessment of Uruguay Round

◆ The failure of GATT members to take adequate account of the likely social and environmental consequences of the Uruguay Round Agreement means that, as an urgent priority, a full impact assessment of the implications and results of the Uruguay Round on the opportunities for sustainable development should be initiated, with particular attention on the impacts on poorer Southern countries.[105] Since the WTO does not have competence in this area, the assessment should be carried out in cooperation with the Commission for Sustainable Development (CSD), and draw on the experience and expertise of all appropriate intergovernmental bodies (including UNEP, UNCTAD, and UNDP), and of NGOs and citizens' groups. Its terms of reference should include, among other things:

- analysis of the effects of the trade liberalisation resulting from the Uruguay Round at local, national, and global levels;
- examination of both the positive and negative effects of the agreement on people's ability to meet social and economic needs, and on the promotion of sustainable development;
- proposals for appropriate responses to observed impacts. This should include any modifications to the Uruguay Round agreements necessary to increase their compatibility with sustainable development.

The assessment should be conducted in two phases:

- an immediate assessment of the likely social and environmental impacts of implementing the Agreement (some of the provisions of which have a significant phase-in period), in order to identify issues of particular concern ;

- an ongoing assessment concurrent with implementation of the Agreement, which monitors impacts based on actual changes in trade flows and on actual application of trade rules, enabling the WTO to respond appropriately to the discovery of negative impacts.

Institutional reform

◆ *Increased Transparency:*[106] The Singapore Ministerial Meeting offers an opportunity to institute concrete steps to improve public participation in the WTO system, with emphasis on open meetings and access to documents, and to make a commitment to incorporate NGO involvement in dispute settlement procedures. Current WTO restrictions on public acccess and disclosure flout Principle 10 of the Rio Declaration on Environment and Development (a document referred to in the Marrakesh Decision on Trade and Environment) which states that environmental issues 'are best handled with the participation of all concerned citizens', and that countries should 'facilitate and encourage public awareness and participation by making information widely available'. A precedent has been set for the successful implementation of these principles in a number of international fora, including the Commission for Sustainable Development (CSD). The CSD restated the need to improve transparency at both its 1994 and 1995 sessions. In its report of the Second Session, it identifies in particular:

the importance of achieving transparency, openness and the active involvement of the public and experts, in relation to work on trade and environment, including work within WTO, UNEP, and UNCTAD, and to dispute settlement processes. The Commission recognises that there is a considerable need for improvement in these areas, and looks forward to the development of specific recommendations in this regard by Governments and the appropriate organisations, in accordance with chapter 38 of Agenda 21. (Chairman's Text on Trade, Environment, and Sustainable Development, 26 May, 1994).

- Governments should therefore support the recent US proposal to allow NGOs to observe committee meetings. This has already been implemented successfully in many meetings of UNEP and the OECD, among others.
- Expanded, timely public access to all documents prepared in connection with WTO dispute resolution cases, as well as panel reports, official reports, negotiating texts, papers related to WTO institutional matters, and notices of dispute challenges, should be introduced.
- The Dispute Settlement system should allow for interventions and submissions by NGOs or international insititutions (for example, UN agencies) with a demonstrated interest in the outcome of cases, including at the appeal stage of the process. Panel rosters for the dispute settlement system should contain ample representation of experts in social and environmental law and policy.
- Governments of the industrialised countries should work to ensure that in future WTO negotiations, developing countries have a greater opportunity to influence the agenda, the negotiations, and the results. Financial and technical assistance for poorer countries to ensure they have effective delegations at the WTO would be helpful.
- *Closer integration into the UN system:* The WTO should be answerable to the United Nations, through regular reports to the Secretary-General, the General Assembly, and the Economic and Social Council. While this would not, in itself, imply a fundamental shift of power and responsibility, it would ensure that international trade issues were debated in a context where the views of small states carry more weight. In all its activities, the WTO should be required to cooperate closely with UN agencies, including the CSD, the ILO, UNDP, UNEP, and UNCTAD.
- *Intergovernmental Panel on Trade and Sustainable Development*: An Intergovernmental Panel on Trade and Sustainable Development (IPTSD) should be established (as set out at the end of chapter three) to provide the WTO environment committee and other institutions with the factual and analytic

foundation for constructive reforms linking trade, environmental protection, and sustainable development.

Other key reforms to make international trade more equitable and sustainable

These include:

- The withdrawal of all discriminatory trade barriers, including tariff and non-tariff measures, targeted at developing countries.

- More effective provision for developing countries to protect fledgling processing and manufacturing industries temporarily, and to diversify out of unsustainable commodity-based exports.

- A comprehensive prohibition of agricultural export subsidisation, and the redesign of agricultural policies in the industrialised countries to encourage less intensive production, and to redistribute income support from the largest producers to small-holders.

- The formulation of rules to forbid countries participating in the multilateral trading system from weakening social and environmental regulations to attract (or retain) new investment.

- The introduction of measures to improve the accountability of TNCs and prevent their activities from eroding people's rights, including the setting up of a global anti-trusts body to recommend and monitor action by governments where markets are distorted by monopoly power. Action is also needed to strengthen governments' ability to prevent transfer pricing, and enforce socially and environmentally responsible patterns of investment through effective codes of conduct. Further expansion of TNC powers under the proposed Multilateral Agreement on Investment should be resisted unless there is a concomitant expansion of TNC responsibilities through the effective international regulation of their social and environmental activities.

◆ Finally, consumers in industrialised countries can play an important role in helping producers to get a fairer return on their labour, by buying fairly-traded products, and by using their power as consumers to put pressure on retailers and suppliers to supply fairly-traded goods, and to adopt and implement independently audited codes of conduct.

Notes

1. Analysis on Chile is drawn from two research reports commissioned by Oxfam: *Flexible Labour Markets, Poverty, and Social Disintegration in Chile*, Fernando Leiva and Rafael Agacino, Chile, 1994, plus update in 1996; and *Impact of the Export Model on Workers and the Environment: Analysis of the Fruit and Fishing Sectors*, Estrella Diaz, ARCIS University, Santiago, Chile, June 1994. See also S Barrientos, 'Flexible Women in Fruit: The "Success" of the Chilean Export Model', University of Hertfordshire, mimeo, 1995.

2. *Restructuring and the New Working Classes in Chile*, Alvaro Diaz, UNRISD, October 1992.

3. According to the Pesticides Action Network.

4. Homeworker, quoted in *Aekta Project Annual Report*, Birmingham, 1995.

5. *Outwork in Leeds: A report by the West Yorkshire Homeworking Unit*, March 1992

6. *The EIU Guide to World Trade under the WTO*, Phillip Evans, James Walsh, Economist Intelligence Unit, London 1995.

7. *Financial Times*, 12 April 1994 and 5 October 1994.

8. *Free Trade: What's In it for Women?* Gillian Moon, Community Aid Abroad, *Background report No 6*, Australia, August 1995

9. Agenda 21 is the global action plan for sustainable development which was agreed at the Rio Earth Summit.

10. F. Schmidt-Bleek and H. Wohlmeyer, *Trade and the Environment: Report on a Study*, Laxenburg, Austria: International Institute for Applied Systems Analysis and the Austrian Association for Agricultural Research, 1991; quoted in Hilary French, *Costly Trade-offs: Reconciling Trade and the Environment, Worldwatch Paper 113*, Washington, March 1993.

11. Lome's central trade provision is the granting of duty-free access to the EU market for most products from the ACP group (African, Caribbean, and Pacific group), subject to certain conditions. See Belinda Coote *The Trade Trap*, Oxfam, 1992. While such trade preferences may not be the most effective way of supporting the livelihoods of poor people, and preferential agreements based on former colonial ties may unfairly exclude other, possibly even poorer nations, withdrawing preferences in the absence of transitional arrangements to protect the poorest groups would impose impose huge social costs.

12 R. Barnet and J. Cavanagh, *Global Dreams: Imperial Corporations and the New World Order*, Simon and Schuster, New York 1994; C. Oman, *Trends in Foreign Direct Investment*, Proceedings of Meeting held on 20 December 1991, Inter-American Development Bank, Washington 1991.

13 Although a national system of royalty collection would also be permitted, its provision is being interpreted very narrowly, and it will probably have to be based on a restrictive model such as the revised UPOV – the International Convention for the Protection of New Varieties of Plants. See *Intellectual Property Rights and the Biodiversity Convention: The Impact of GATT*, Friends of the Earth, London, 1994, and *The UN Biodiversity Convention and the WTO TRIPS Agreement*, WWF International Discussion Paper, Gland, Switzerland 1995.

14 See Jeff Atkinson, *GATT: What do the Poor Get?*, Community Aid Abroad *Background Report 5*, Australia, September 1994.

15 FoE: *Intellectual Property Rights and the Biodiversity Convention: The Impact of GATT*, op cit.1994.

16 Sir Leon Brittan *A Level Playing Field for Direct Investment Worldside*, Communication presented by the European Commission, 1995.

17 *Agreement on Trade Related Investment Measures*, WTO, *Article 9*.

18 Evans, Walsh, op cit.

19 See useful briefing on this issue by Benchmark Environmental Consulting, Portland, ME, USA December 1995.

20 Steve Charnovitz 'The WTO and social issues', *Journal of World Trade*, October 1994.

21 WTO Agreement, *Preamble*.

22 Coats Viyella, Britain's largest textile firm, recently announced that it will shift more production to low-cost countries, following a 6.2 per cent fall in profits for 1995. *The Guardian*, 15 March 1996.

23 *Free Labour World*, January 1996.

24 *The Financial Express*, Dhaka, 24 February 1996.

25 The USA is still the main market for Bangladeshi exports of all types, with about one-third going to the EU.

26 'Export Prospect for Ready Made Garment Industry', Draft final report, November 1993, Rahman Rahman Huq, Chartered Accountants, Dhaka.

27 M. Bhuiyan 'The textile and clothing industry in Bangladesh', *EIU Textile Outlook International*, March 1991, 57-75.

28 Abu Taher, former Vice President of the Bangladesh Garment Manufacturers' and Exporters' Association (BGMEA) – interview with Oxfam, November 1995.

29 See discussion on MFA, chapter one, p.15.

30 S. Feldman, 'Crisis, Islam, and gender in Bangladesh: the social construction of a female labour force', in L. Beneria and S. Feldman (eds) *Unequal Burden*, Boulder, Westview Press, USA 1992. Quoted by Diane Elson, *Uneven Development and the Textiles and Clothing Industry*, Women Working Worldwide, Manchester, 1994.

31 This is not to be interpreted as an argument for maintaining the MFA, which was arbitrary and discriminatory, and probably cost developing countries as a whole $50 billion/year. It is, however, an argument for special treatment for the poorest countries, like Bangladesh, who are likely to suffer in the short term from its removal.

32 Mr. Taher, as above, note 28.

33 Interview with Prof. Hafiz Siddiqui, *Financial Express*, Dhaka, June 13, 1995.

34 'Export Prospect for Ready Made Garment Industry', Draft final report, November 1993, Rahman Rahman Huq, Chartered Accountants, Dhaka.

35 £1 = Taka 63, in December 1995.

36 See Susan Joekes, *Trade-related Employment for Women in Industry and Services in Developing Countries*, UNRISD/UNDP Occasional Paper, 1995, pp.44-45.

37 Mashuda Khatun Shefali, Director of garment working women hostel project of Nari Uddog Kendra, Dhaka.

38 'Trade liberalisation policies and impact on women working in the Export Processing Zone in Bangladesh: a case study', Nilufar Ahmed, Khushi Kabir, in *Proceedings of the Regional Seminar on Global Trading Practices and Poverty Alleviation in South Asia: A Gender Perspective*, India, 1995.

39 Diane Elson, op cit.

40 Ahmed and Kabir, op cit. Their findings are supported both by Oxfam's own findings, and by research by the Clean Clothes Campaign in 1995. See also *Socio-Economic Conditions of the Female Workers Engaged in the Garment Industry in Bangladesh*, Bangladesh Institute of Development Studies, Mirpur, 1993.

41 Hameeda Hossain, 'Surviving economic integration: can women cross the border to security?' in *Proceedings of the Regional Seminar on Global*

Trading Practices and Poverty Alleviation in South Asia: A Gender Perspective, India, 1995.

42 Clean Clothes Campaign Research, SOMO, The Netherlands, 1996.

43 In 1974, 22 companies employed just over 5000 people; by 1994, over 400 companies employed over 140,000 people. See *The Situation of Women in Free Trade Zones*, Dr. Karyma Marra, DR, June 1994; Oxfam Caribbe-CONSA 1989, FUNDAPEC, *Survey of Labour* December 1992, and *National Survey 1991*.

44 Interview with National Garment Workers' Federation, *Financial Express*, Dhaka, Sept.4th, 1995.

45 See p. 49-51 for a further discussion of child labour.

46 In 1995 Oxfam launched its Campaign for Basic Rights. Within the overall framework of this long-term Campaign, activities will focus on particular aspects of denial of rights. Thus, in May 1996, Oxfam launched the Clothes Campaign, to demonstrate the extent to which the right to a livelihood is jeopardised by exploitative conditions for workers in the garments industry.

47 Contact Clean Clothes Campaign for further information: van Ostadestraat 233b, 1073 TN Amsterdam, The Netherlands. The UK arm of the Campaign, which involves a number of UK NGOs including Oxfam, can be contacted at Label Behind the Labour, c/o Women Working Worldwide, Centre for Employment Research, Room 3, St. Augustines Building, Lower Chatham St, Manchester M15 6BY. Recently an international campaign linking The World Development Movement, The Trades Union Congress, and the Catholic Institute for International Relations in Britain with toy worker groups in SE Asia and with the ICFTU has been set up to press transnational toy companies to adopt an independently monitored 'Charter on the Safe Production of Toys'. It has already had some success. An international campaign focusing on the working conditions in sports shoe factories is also underway.

48 This is based on a code of conduct devised by the Fair Trade Foundation, and forms the core of several codes currently being used by NGOs and consumer groups to effect change in the garments and sports shoe industries.

49 The focus of this report is on the possibilities for international regulation. A forthcoming report from Oxfam will explore the role of government and World Bank/IMF policies on employment conditions.

50 *ILO Digest*.

51 ILO Governing Body, 1994.

52 ILO Governing Body, GB.264/6, Geneva, November 1995.

53 Gijsbert van Liemt, Senior Economist, ILO, 'How operational would a multilateral social clause be?' Paper given at International Seminar on Trade, Aid, and Minimum Labour Standards: Visions and Campaigns from the South and the North, Amsterdam, May 1994.

54 Robert Plant, *Labour Standards and Structural Adjustment*, ILO, Geneva, 1994.

55 See footnote 49.

56 See Anti-Slavery International *Briefing Notes, World Trade and Working Children*, London, September 1995.

57 ILO GB.264//ESP/1, Geneva November 1995; also Simon Steyne, TUC, pers.comm.

58 See position paper *Why GATT and the WTO Should Not Deal with Labour Standards*, Martin Khor, Third World Network, Malaysia April 1994.

59 Jagdish Bhagwati, 'A View from academia' in *International Labor Standards and the Global Economic Integration*, US Deparment of Labor, July 1994.

60 Khor, op cit.

61 *Financial Times*, 14 June 1995

62 UK Prime Minister John Major, quoted in *The Guardian*, 13 March 1996.

63 ICFTU, 'Submission to the Negotiators Preparing the Final Agreement of the Uruguay Round of the GATT Multilateral Trade Negotiations', undated.

64 Ruth Mayne, 'Adjustment and small businesses', *Appropriate Technology* 22: 3, December 1995.

65 Angela Hale, *World Trade is a Women's Issue*, Women Working Worldwide, Manchester 1996.

66 ICFTU *Position Paper*, Brussels 1993. See also position paper from the International Textile, Garment and Leather Workers Federation, *Enabling Workers to Share the Benefits of World Trade*.

67 Governing Body, International Labour Office, *The Social Dimensions of the Liberalisation of World Trade*, GB.261/WP/SLD/1, 261st Session, Geneva, November 1994.

68 These proposals are from Michel Hansenne, Director General, ILO, in document cited above.

69 *NAFTA's First Year: Lessons for the Hemisphere*, ed. Sarah Anderson, John Cavanagh, David Ranney, Paul Schwab, AUS Citizens Analysis, December 1994.

70 Stephen Woolcock, *The Trade and Labour Standards Debate: Overburdening or Defending the Multilateral System? Global Economic Institutions Working Paper Series*, 4. ESRC, December 1995.

71 ibid.

72 Pharis J. Harvey, *US GSP Labour Rights Conditionality: 'Aggressive Unilateralism' or A Forerunner to a Multilateral Social Clause?*, International Labour Rights Fund, Washington, USA, October 1995.

73 Woolcock, op. cit.

74 Harvey, op cit.

75 Steve Charnovitz, 'The WTO and social issues', *Journal of World Trade*, October 1994.

76 Quoted in Duncan Green, *Silent Revolution: The Rise of Market Economics in Latin America*, Cassell, and Latin American Bureau, London, 1995.

77 Hilary French, *Costly Trade-offs: Reconciling Trade and the Environment*, op cit 1993.

78 ibid.

79 Extract from testimony of Alma Molina, maquiladora worker, quoted in Belinda Coote, *NAFTA*, Oxfam 1995.

80 'German chemical giants target China', *Financial Times*, 25 January 1994; Shanghai alone has attracted 120 of the world's largest 500 TNCs. See UNCTAD, *World Investment Report 1994*.

81 Governments are less likely to enact legislation to improve environmental standards if they are presented with the threat that industry will relocate to areas of lower standards as a result; similarly, workers are less likely to push for higher standards if they fear their jobs are at risk.

82 Daniel Esty, *Greening the GATT: Trade, Environment, and the Future*, Institute for International Economics, Washington DC, 1994.

83 Esty, op cit.

84 Bhagwati, J (1993) *The Case For Free Trade*, Scientific American.

85 Paul Ekins, *Harnessing Trade to Sustainable Development*, Green College Centre for Environmental Policy and Understanding, Oxford, March 1995.

86 See Paul Ekins' discussion of the Kuznets Curve, op cit. and also Dieneke Ferguson et al, *Dangerous Curves: Does the Environment Inprove*

with Economic Growth?, WWF International Research Report, Gland Switzerland, February 1996.

87 The EC Task Force on the Single Market, for example, predicted that cross border traffic would grow by 30-50 per cent with the opening of Europe's borders in 1993. Air traffic is expected to increase at an even higher rate. The energy costs associated with such increases are massive. Transporting the 4 billion tons of freight sent by ship worldwide in 1991 required 8.1 exajoules of energy – as much as was used by the entire economies of Brazil and Turkey combined. See Hilary French, *Costly Tradeoffs: Reconciling Trade and the Environment*, op. cit.1993.

88 Task Force on Environment and the Internal Market, *'1992': The Environmental Dimension*, Bonn: Economica Verlag, 1990.

89 OECD, *The Environmental Effects of Trade*, Paris 1994.

90 Charnovitz, op. cit.

91 Significantly, the recent US-Venezuela panel on reformulated gasoline did in fact classify a clean atmosphere as an exhaustible natural resource.

93 Dan Esty has proposed a Green Fund, to be financed by 1/100 of 1 per cent tax on trade and capital flows, which could generate $15-$20 billion/year.

94 See *Taxes for Environmental Purposes: The Scope for Border Tax Adjustment under WTO Rules*, WWF International Discussion Paper, Gland, Switzerland, October 1995.

95 Paul Ekins, op cit

96 Duncan Brack, 'International affairs', *RIIA*, Vol.71, 1995, p.506.

97 For related ideas, see Paul Ekins, *Harnessing Trade to Sustainable Development*, Green College Centre for Environmental Policy and Understanding, March, 1995 p.7; NRDC/Field, Environmental Priorities for the World Trading System; Brack, op cit.

98 There could be various ways of defining 'significant': for example, it could derive from the impact on local communities or be calculated in economic terms in terms of resource depreciation.

99 The lack of an environmental body with a parallel power and authority over environment issues to balance the WTO's authority over trade issues is keenly felt. Some analysts have called for the creation of a new Global Environmental Organisation to fill this gap (e.g. Esty, op cit). However, while this may be desirable, its feasibility seems a very long way off.

100 James Cameron, Halina Ward, and Zen Mazuch, *Sustainable Development and Integrated Dispute Settlement in GATT, 1994*, WWF International Discussion Paper, Gland, Switzerland.

101 Iman Ali Shardar, Khulna district, interview with author, March 1995.

102 See *Yellow Fever: A Proposal for Quota Allocation for Fair Trade Bananas*, Euroban and Solidaridad, The Netherlands, 1995.

103 This section draws on analysis by WWF International. See 'Intergovernmental Panel on Trade and Sustainable Development', in *Making UNCED Work*, Gland, Switzerland, October 1994.

104 See *Sustainable Development and the Possibilities for the Reflection of Environmental Costs in Prices*, UNCTAD Secretariat, TD/B/ CN.1/29 August 1995).

105 See *Terms of Reference for an Assessment: Impact of the Uruguay Round on Environment and Sustainable Development*, WWF International, Gland, Switzerland, October 1994.

106 These recommendations draw on: *Environmental Priorities for the World Trading System*, Natural Resources Defense Council and Foundation for International Environmental Law and Development, January 1995)

Oxfam Insight

Other books in the Oxfam Insight series

The **Insight** series offers concise and accessible analysis of issues that are of current concern to the international community.

Paying for Health: Poverty and Structural Adjustment in Zimbabwe

Jean Lennock
ISBN 0 85598 293 4, 40 pages, 1994

Jean Lennock shows how the most vulnerable sections of society carry the burden of structural adjustment when a government adopts the World Bank's advice to introduce user-fees for health care.

Rwanda: An Agenda for International Action

Guy Vassall-Adams
ISBN 0 85598 299 3, 72 pages, 1994

Guy Vassall-Adams investigates the background to the genocide and refugee crisis which devastated Rwanda in 1994, and explores the reasons why the international community intervened too late to prevent the tragedy. The book argues for radical reform and proper funding of the UN's peacekeeping and emergency capacities, and presents specific recommendations for action.

A Case for Reform: Fifty Years of the IMF and World Bank

Oxfam Policy Department
ISBN 0 85598 301 9, 64 pages, 1994

The World Bank and the International Monetary Fund dominate the economic policy-making of many of the world's poorest countries. Fifty years after they were created, what impact have they had on the ordinary people's lives? **A Case for Reform** argues that the free-market ideology of these undemocratic institutions has actually added to the poverty of many communities. It calls for a fundamental review of their policies and a radical reform of their operations, and makes recommendations for international action.

NAFTA: Poverty and Free Trade in Mexico

Belinda Coote
ISBN 0 85598 302 7, 64 pages, 1995

The North American Free Trade Agreement, the first economic treaty to unite developed and developing countries, has created the largest free-trade zone in the world. Will it lead to prosperity for all in Mexico, or will it leave the country open to exploitation and unfair competition? This book examines the lessons to be learned from the NAFTA experience by other poor countries experimenting with policies of economic liberalisation.

Oxfam (UK and Ireland) publishes a wide range of books, manuals, and resource materials for specialist, academic, and general readers. For a free catalogue, please write to Oxfam Publishing, Oxfam House, 274 Banbury Road, Oxford, OX2 7DZ, UK.

INSIGHT BOOKS are produced by Oxfam UK and Ireland as part of its advocacy programme on behalf of poor communities. They are co-published with other members of the international Oxfam group. For more information, contact your National Oxfam:

Oxfam America
25 West Street
Boston MA 0211 1206
USA
Tel: 1 617 482 1211
Fax: 1 617 728 2594

Oxfam Canada
Suite 300
294 Albert Street
Ottawa, Ontario K1P 6E6
Canada
Tel: 1 613 237 5236
Fax: 1 613 237 0524

Community Aid Abroad
156 George Street
Fitzroy
Victoria
Australia
Tel: 61 3 289 9444
Fax: 61 3 419 5318

Oxfam New Zealand
Room 101, La Gonda House
203 Karangahape Road
Auckland, New Zealand
Tel: 64 9 358 1480
Fax: 64 9 358 1481

Oxfam Hong Kong
Ground Floor 3B
June Garden
28 Tung Chau Street
Tai Kok Tsui
Kowloon, Hong Kong
Tel: 852 3 916305
Fax: 852 789 9545

The international Oxfams are a group of autonomous, non-profit development agencies. They work to overcome poverty and social injustice through the empowerment of partner organisations and communities to achieve sustainable development or livelihoods, and to strengthen civil society in any part of the world, irrespective of nationality, race, political system, religion, or colour. They are Oxfam America, Oxfam Belgique/Belgie, Oxfam Canada, Community Aid Abroad (in Australia), Oxfam Hong Kong, NOVIB (in the Netherlands), Oxfam Quebec, and Oxfam United Kingdom and Ireland. The name Oxfam comes from the OXford Committee for FAMine relief, founded in Oxford, England in 1942.

Insight books are available through Oxfam UK and Ireland's book distributors.